The

NO-SHOP INSTANT POT®

240 OPTIONS

for Amazing Meals with Ingredients
You Already Have

MEG DOW

Creator of More Momma

PAGE STREET
PUBLISHING CO.

PAGE STREET
PUBLISHING CO.

First published in 2021 by
Page Street Publishing Co.
27 Congress Street, Suite 105
Salem, MA 01970
www.pagestreetpublishing.com

Distributed by Macmillan, sales in Canada by The Canadian Manda Group.

25   24   23   22   21   1   2   3   4   5

ISBN-13: 978-1-64567-253-1
ISBN-10: 1-64567-253-0

Library of Congress Control Number: 2020942653

Cover and book design by Meg Baskis for Page Street Publishing Co.
Photography by Becky Winkler

Printed and bound in China

Instant Pot® is a registered trademark of Double Insight, Inc., which was not involved in the creation of this book.

THIS BOOK IS DEDICATED TO MY FAMILY.

You are the reason why I value family mealtime and strive to get meals on the table. I love you to eternity and beyond!

CONTENTS

INTRODUCTION

Hi, friend!

I am Meg, an Italian-trained chef and momma of three. I value family dinner so much that it is ranked as one of the most important times of the day for my family. So much goodness can come from sitting and eating together.

Realistically, dinnertime, or any mealtime for that matter, can be the most stressful time of the day. From all of the extracurricular activities, children needing to be held and the rush to feed all of the hungry mouths, I need quick and easy recipes to make dinnertime a success. Even more, I need recipes that don't take a lot of my time sitting in front of the stove or tending to things in the oven.

That is where the Instant Pot® comes into play. The Instant Pot is my go-to cooking vessel when the craziness of life tries to overrun my family dinner goal. I love that the Instant Pot cooks without me needing to be its babysitter, because, let's face it, I already have three children to babysit.

The recipes you'll find in this book are all made with ingredients you probably already have on hand. Each base recipe has four different variations, so if you don't have the ingredients for one variation, chances are you probably will have the ingredients for one of the other three. It makes it really easy to find tasty recipes that use ingredients that you already have in your kitchen.

The infographics found in each recipe can also help you to find a variation that uses ingredients you already have with one quick glance. You can easily see the different options and compare them to what ingredients you have handy in your pantry and fridge.

When talking to my readers or followers on social media, most people are intimidated by the Instant Pot. Heck, some people may have not taken it out of the box just yet. That's okay! I will teach you all the basics plus answer the most frequently asked questions about the Instant Pot, and you will be crushing your dinnertime goals with this handy machine by the end of it!

INSTANT POT BASICS

USING LIQUID IN THE INSTANT POT

ALWAYS add liquid to the insert. The amount of water or liquid will be included in the recipe.

RELEASING PRESSURE

There are a couple of different methods to release the pressure that builds up while cooking with the Instant Pot. I will tell you exactly how to release the pressure in the directions since it will affect the cooking and doneness of the dishes.

QUICK RELEASE

When releasing the pressure by a quick release, you will be manually releasing the pressure by carefully moving the pressure valve to the venting position. You want to do this with a kitchen towel or an oven mitt since the steam will release from the valve and can burn you. Also do not put your face anywhere near the valve.

NATURAL RELEASE

When releasing the pressure naturally, you will not move the valve at all. It will automatically start to depressurize. When you see the red pin drop it means all the pressure has been released and you can open the lid. This takes about 10 to 20 minutes to do naturally, depending on how much pressure has built up.

NATURAL RELEASE AND THEN QUICK RELEASE

For this method you will want to start a timer once the Instant Pot beeps after it is finished cooking. Set the timer for the natural release time. Once the time is up, you can manually perform the quick release by moving the valve to the venting position. This method is used for things like rice where it can create a better finished product if the pressure is released slowly. I also like to use this sometimes for pasta recipes since it can spew out cooking liquid (rather than just the steam) from the valve. If this does happen, you can throw a paper towel over the valve to catch any cooking liquid and just wash the lid thoroughly.

POT-IN-POT METHOD

The pot-in-pot method is simply using another pot within the Instant Pot insert. A lot of the recipes in this book use this method. I like to cover the food with a paper towel first and then with foil. The paper towel catches excess steam and will keep your dish from getting soggy.

When cooking with pots within the Instant Pot you will want to use a pan that is oven-safe and that fits in your Instant Pot.

INSTANT POT FAQS

WHAT ARE THE ESSENTIAL TOOLS I NEED FOR THE INSTANT POT?

- 2 sealing rings (one for sweet dishes and one for savory dishes)
- Cake pan (that fits the size of your insert)
- For the pot-in-pot method, you can use a high trivet
- Silicone mini muffin mold
- Steamer basket
- Trivet

WHAT IF I HAVE AN OLDER OR NEWER MODEL OF THE INSTANT POT AND DON'T HAVE THE SAME BUTTONS AS THE RECIPE STATES?

There are many models of Instant Pots on the market. If you are reading any of the recipes and can't find a manual button, use the pressure level button, press for high or low pressure and then adjust the time with the + or - button. In some models you will need to press the start button and in some models it automatically turns on after you have pressed manual pressure and plugged in the allotted time.

HOW DO YOU USE THE SAUTÉ BUTTON?

Quite a few of these recipes require the sauté button, which every Instant Pot should have. Simply press the sauté button and wait until the pot reads HOT before you start the recipe. When switching modes of cooking from sauté to manual you will need to press the keep warm/cancel button to switch modes.

WHAT ABOUT ALL THE PRE-PROGRAMMED BUTTONS?

I do not recommend using the pre-programmed buttons since cooking different rice or stews will take different amounts of time. Just follow the times in the recipes.

I FOLLOWED THE RECIPE BUT MY DISH IS NOT COOKED FULLY—WHAT DO I DO?

In some instances, recipes can cook differently. If your dish is not fully cooked just put the lid back on and cook for an additional amount of time. This can happen especially with things like chicken or baked potatoes. If you have a large chicken breast it may take a little longer than the recipe states. Don't worry! Just place the lid back on and cook for an additional 5 minutes, or until it's cooked through.

HOW DO I CLEAN THE INSTANT POT?

The Instant Pot is actually very easy to clean. You can clean the lid and the insert under hot soapy water and then put it in the dishwasher. Place the insert on the bottom rack and the lid on the top rack.

If you do not have an extra sealing ring, you can wash the insert and lid through the dishwasher and then place 1 cup (240 ml) of water in the insert with 2 tablespoons (8 g) of ground cinnamon. Seal the valve and press manual, high pressure for 5 minutes. Remove and rinse out. You can now use the pot for sweet dishes.

WHY DID I GET A BURN NOTICE?

You should not have a burn notice on your Instant Pot if you follow the directions. The Instant Pot requires liquid (such as water) to create steam and pressure to cook the food. When the steam evaporates too quickly or if there is not enough water in the pot, you will get a burn notice.

DINNER

I know, I know, dinnertime can be one of the more stressful times of the day. But I promise these recipes will help get dinner on the table quickly and easily. Alfredo Pasta Shells (page 41) take only 2 minutes to cook. Pickle Ranch Chuck Roast (page 16) can be made in half the time in the Instant Pot and Citrus Carnitas Pork Shoulder (page 33) is made in a quarter of the time from that of a traditional carnitas recipe.

If there is one thing that I love about the Instant Pot, it's that I can throw everything into the pot and have dinner on the table for my family without thinking. These dinner recipes include pot-in-pot recipes—where you will use multiple pots within the Instant Pot to have your main dish and sides all done at once—along with easy dump and go recipes that take little to no effort at all.

The best part of utilizing the Instant Pot for dinner is that there are minimal dishes! Less mess = more time to spend with your family.

CHUCK ROAST

YIELD: 6 SERVINGS

Chuck roast is one of my favorite Instant Pot dinners. It becomes
mouthwateringly tender and shreddable and is perfect for a cold winter night.
My favorite chuck roast has to be the Pickle Ranch Chuck Roast (page 16). It
may sound a little out there, but it's delicious!

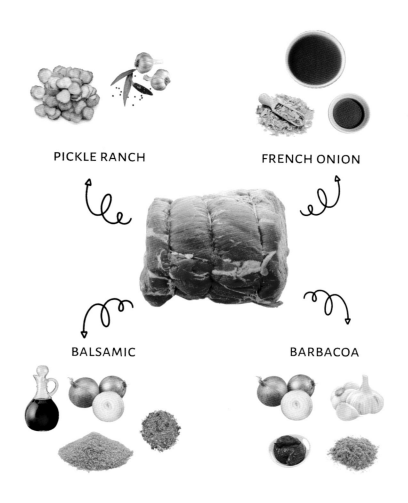

PICKLE RANCH

FRENCH ONION

BALSAMIC

BARBACOA

PICKLE RANCH CHUCK ROAST

4 lbs (1.8 kg) boneless chuck roast, cut into 3-inch (8-cm) strips

1 tbsp (15 ml) avocado or olive oil

1 cup (240 ml) good quality pickle juice, such as Grillo's Pickles

1 cup (145 g) good quality pickle chips

1 packet (28 g) dry ranch dip mix

Turn the Instant Pot on to sauté mode. Pat the chuck roast dry with a paper towel to remove excess moisture. Add the oil and 3 strips of meat to the Instant Pot. Sear about 5 minutes per side until browned. Remove and set aside. Finish browning the rest of the meat and then add it back into the Instant Pot insert along with the pickle juice, pickle chips and ranch dip mix.

Seal the lid and turn the valve to the sealing position. Turn the Instant Pot on manual, high pressure for 60 minutes. Release the pressure manually by carefully moving the valve to venting. Shred the meat and serve over the starch of your choice.

NOTE

This goes perfectly on top of Mashed Potatoes (page 197) or even in sandwiches.

See image on page 14.

FRENCH ONION CHUCK ROAST

4 lbs (1.8 kg) boneless chuck roast, cut into 3-inch (8-cm) strips

2 tsp (12 g) kosher salt

½ tsp black pepper

1 tbsp (15 ml) avocado or olive oil

1 oz (28 g) packet French onion dip mix

2 tbsp (30 ml) Worcestershire sauce

1 cup (240 ml) beef stock

Turn the Instant Pot on to sauté mode. Pat the chuck roast dry with a paper towel to remove excess moisture. Season the chuck roast with salt and pepper. Add the oil and 3 strips of meat to the Instant Pot. Sear about 5 minutes per side until browned. Remove and set aside. Finish browning the rest of the meat and then add it back into the Instant Pot insert along with the French onion dip mix, Worcestershire sauce and stock.

Seal the lid and turn the valve to the sealing position. Turn the Instant Pot on manual, high pressure for 60 minutes. Release the pressure manually by carefully moving the valve to venting. Shred the meat before serving.

NOTE

This goes perfectly in sandwiches with some good quality pickles and buttered toasted rolls. Save the extra cooking liquid for dipping like with a French dip sandwich.

BALSAMIC CHUCK ROAST

4 lbs (1.8 kg) boneless chuck roast, cut into 3-inch (8-cm) strips

1 tbsp (15 ml) avocado or olive oil

2 cups (230 g) white onion, sliced thinly

½ cup (120 ml) balsamic vinegar

¼ cup (55 g) and 1 tbsp (14 g) brown sugar, divided

2 tsp (2 g) Italian seasoning

¼ cup (60 ml) water

1 tsp kosher salt

1 tbsp (8 g) cornstarch mixed with 1 tbsp (15 ml) cold water

Turn the Instant Pot on to sauté mode. Pat the chuck roast dry with a paper towel to remove excess moisture. Add the oil and 3 strips of meat to the Instant Pot. Sear about 5 minutes per side until browned. Remove and set aside. Finish browning the rest of the meat and then add it back into the Instant Pot insert along with the onion, vinegar, ¼ cup (55 g) brown sugar, Italian seasoning and water.

Seal the lid and turn the valve to the sealing position. Turn the Instant Pot on manual, high pressure for 60 minutes. Release the pressure manually by carefully moving the valve to venting. Shred the meat and add the salt, cornstarch mixture and 1 tablespoon (14 g) of brown sugar.

NOTE

This is the perfect Sunday roast to top creamy Mashed Potatoes (page 197).

BARBACOA CHUCK ROAST

4 lbs (1.8 kg) boneless chuck roast, cut into 3-inch (8-cm) strips

1 tbsp (15 ml) avocado or olive oil

½ cup (80 g) white onion, diced

1 tbsp (9 g) minced garlic, about 3 cloves

1 tsp kosher salt

⅛ tsp black pepper

1 tsp garlic salt

¼ tsp ground cumin

1 tsp onion powder

1 tbsp (17 g) chipotle chili in adobo, roughly chopped

½ cup (120 ml) beef broth

Turn the Instant Pot on to sauté mode. Pat the chuck roast dry with a paper towel to remove excess moisture. Add the oil and 3 strips of meat to the Instant Pot. Sear about 5 minutes per side until browned. Remove and set aside. Finish browning the rest of the meat and then add it back into the Instant Pot insert along with the onion, garlic, salt, pepper, garlic salt, cumin, onion powder, chipotle and broth.

Seal the lid and turn the valve to the sealing position. Turn the Instant Pot on manual, high pressure for 60 minutes. Release the pressure manually by carefully moving the valve to venting. Shred the meat before serving.

CHICKEN BREAST

YIELD: 4 SERVINGS

These delicious chicken recipes can be served over rice or pasta
and are perfect for a quick, easy dinner that the whole family will enjoy.
Our go-to recipe is the Salsa-Ranch Chicken (page 20), which goes perfectly
on top of nachos, in burritos, rice bowls or just on its own.

COCONUT, MANGO AND LIME   SALSA-RANCH

ARTICHOKE-BACON   CREAM OF MUSHROOM
AND SHERRY

COCONUT, MANGO AND LIME CHICKEN

1 tbsp (15 ml) avocado or olive oil

2 lbs (907 g) boneless, skinless chicken breasts, sliced into thin 1-inch (3-cm) strips

1 (13.5-oz [382-g]) can of coconut milk

2 cups (280 g) frozen diced mango

1½ tsp (9 g) kosher salt

1 tbsp (8 g) cornstarch combined with 2 tbsp (30 ml) water

2 tsp (8 g) brown sugar

Zest of 1 lime

2 tsp (4 g) curry powder

4 cups (744 g) cooked jasmine rice, for serving

Lime wedges, for garnish

Turn the Instant Pot on to sauté mode and add the oil. Add the chicken and sauté in batches so as not to overcrowd the pot for 5 to 7 minutes. Add the coconut milk and mango and stir to combine. Seal the lid and turn the valve to the sealing position. Turn the Instant Pot on manual, high pressure for 5 minutes. Let the pressure release naturally for 5 minutes. Remove any excess pressure by carefully moving the valve to venting. Turn the Instant Pot on to sauté mode and add the salt, cornstarch mixture, brown sugar, lime zest and curry powder. Simmer for 3 minutes to thicken. Serve over rice and garnish with lime wedges.

See image on page 18.

SALSA-RANCH CHICKEN

½ cup (120 ml) water

2 lbs (907 g) boneless, skinless chicken breasts

1 (12-oz [340-g]) jar of mild red salsa

1 (1-oz [28-g]) packet dry ranch dip mix

8 oz (226 g) cream cheese, cut into large cubes

1 (15-oz [425-g]) can of black beans, drained and rinsed

1 (8-oz [226-g]) can of corn, drained and rinsed

4 cups (744 g) cooked jasmine rice, for serving

Place the water and chicken in the bottom of the Instant Pot insert. Top with the salsa and ranch dip mix. Seal the lid and turn the valve to the sealing position. Turn the Instant Pot on manual, high pressure for 17 minutes. Manually release the pressure by carefully moving the valve to venting. Add the cream cheese, beans and corn and turn on to sauté mode. Stir to melt the cream cheese. Serve over rice.

CREAM OF MUSHROOM AND SHERRY CHICKEN

2 tbsp (28 g) unsalted butter

2 cloves garlic, minced

1½ cups (115 g) sliced button or cremini mushrooms

½ cup (120 ml) cooking sherry

2 lbs (907 g) boneless, skinless chicken breasts

2 (10.5-oz [298-g]) cans of cream of mushroom soup, or homemade Cream of Chicken and Mushroom Soup (page 86)

Kosher salt and pepper, to taste

1 lb (454 g) cooked egg noodles, for serving

Turn the Instant Pot on to sauté mode. Add the butter, garlic and mushrooms and sauté for 5 minutes, stirring occasionally. Add the sherry and stir to pull up any bits stuck to the bottom. Top the mushrooms with the chicken. Seal the lid and turn the valve to the sealing position. Turn the Instant Pot on manual, high pressure for 17 minutes. Manually release the pressure by carefully moving the valve to venting. Stir in the cream of mushroom soup and season with salt and pepper to taste. Serve the chicken over the egg noodles.

ARTICHOKE-BACON CHICKEN

2 lbs (907 g) boneless, skinless chicken breasts

Kosher salt and black pepper, to taste

1½ cups (360 ml) white cooking wine

1 (14-oz [396-g]) can of artichoke hearts, drained and roughly chopped

4 slices of bacon, cooked until crispy, roughly chopped

2 cups (226 g) shredded cheddar cheese

1 lb (454 g) cooked egg noodles, for serving

Place the chicken in the bottom of the Instant Pot insert. Season the chicken with salt and pepper to taste. Add the wine and artichoke hearts. Seal the lid and turn the valve to the sealing position. Turn the Instant Pot on manual, high pressure for 17 minutes. Manually release the pressure by carefully moving the valve to venting. Top the chicken with the bacon and cheddar cheese and cover with the lid. Let sit for 5 minutes to melt the cheese. Serve the chicken over the egg noodles.

CHICKEN THIGHS

YIELD: 4 SERVINGS

Chicken thighs are ideal for Instant Pot cooking. They come out perfectly cooked, tender and moist. You can also use skinless thighs for these recipes. The Chicken Thighs with Orange-Fig Sauce (page 25) is great for a week-night meal and elegant enough to serve for company.

ORANGE FIG

HERB-CRUSTED WITH GRAVY

CREAMY TARRAGON

PORTUGUESE

HERB-CRUSTED CHICKEN THIGHS WITH GRAVY

4 bone-in, skin-on chicken thighs
1 tsp kosher salt
⅛ tsp black pepper
2 tsp (2 g) minced fresh sage
2 tsp (2 g) minced fresh rosemary
¼ cup (31 g) plus 1 tbsp (8 g) all-purpose flour, divided
3 tbsp (42 g) unsalted butter
1 cup (240 ml) chicken stock
2 tsp (5 g) cornstarch mixed with 1 tbsp (15 ml) cold water
4 cups (744 g) cooked jasmine rice, for serving

Season the chicken with the salt, pepper and herbs. Dredge the chicken in ¼ cup (31 g) of flour. Turn the Instant Pot on to sauté mode. Add the butter to melt. Add the chicken and sauté in batches so as not to overcrowd the pot for 5 to 7 minutes, skin side down. Flip the chicken and sprinkle the remaining tablespoon (8 g) of flour into the pan and stir. Add the stock and cover with the lid. Seal the lid and turn the valve to the sealing position.

Turn the Instant Pot on manual, high pressure for 20 minutes. Manually release the pressure by carefully moving the valve to venting.

Remove the chicken, reserving the juices in the Instant Pot insert, and place it on a foil-lined baking sheet. Place the chicken under the broiler for 5 minutes to brown.

Turn the Instant Pot on to sauté mode and add the cornstarch mixture. Simmer the gravy for 3 minutes to thicken. Season with salt and pepper to taste. Pour the gravy over the chicken. Serve the chicken over the rice.

See image on page 22.

PORTUGUESE CHICKEN THIGHS

1 tbsp (14 g) unsalted butter
7 oz (198 g) Portuguese sausage, sliced into ¼-inch (6-mm) slices
½ cup (57 g) yellow onion, sliced thinly
4 bone-in, skin-on chicken thighs
1 tsp kosher salt
⅛ tsp black pepper
¼ cup (31 g) all-purpose flour
1 tsp garlic salt
½ tsp smoked paprika
1 tbsp (8 g) garlic, minced
3 cups (438 g) baby Dutch potatoes
1 (14.5-oz [411-g]) can diced tomatoes
4 cups (744 g) cooked jasmine rice, for serving

Turn the Instant Pot on to sauté mode. Add the butter to melt. Add the sausage and onion and sauté for 3 to 4 minutes. Season the chicken with the salt and pepper. Dredge the seasoned chicken in the flour. Add the chicken to the pot and sauté in batches so as not to overcrowd the pot for 5 to 7 minutes, skin side down. Flip the chicken and add the garlic salt, paprika, minced garlic, potatoes and tomatoes. Seal the lid and turn the valve to the sealing position. Turn the Instant Pot on manual, high pressure for 20 minutes. Manually release the pressure by carefully moving the valve to venting. Serve the chicken over the rice.

CREAMY TARRAGON CHICKEN THIGHS

1 tbsp (14 g) unsalted butter
½ cup (57 g) yellow onion, sliced thinly
4 bone-in, skin-on chicken thighs
1 tsp kosher salt
⅛ tsp black pepper
¼ cup (31 g) all-purpose flour
1 tsp garlic salt
1 cup (240 ml) white cooking wine
¼ cup (60 ml) heavy cream
1 tbsp (1 g) tarragon leaves, roughly chopped
1 lb (454 g) cooked egg noodles, for serving

Turn the Instant Pot on to sauté mode. Add the butter to melt. Add the onion and sauté for 3 to 4 minutes. Season the chicken with the salt and pepper. Dredge the seasoned chicken in the flour. Add the chicken to the pot and sauté in batches so as not to overcrowd the pot for 5 to 7 minutes, skin side down. Flip the chicken and add the garlic salt and wine. Seal the lid and turn the valve to the sealing position. Turn the Instant Pot on manual, high pressure for 20 minutes. Manually release the pressure by carefully moving the valve to venting. Remove the chicken and shred. Return the chicken to the pot and add the cream and tarragon. Serve the chicken over the egg noodles.

CHICKEN THIGHS WITH ORANGE-FIG SAUCE

1 tbsp (14 g) unsalted butter
4 bone-in, skin-on chicken thighs
1 tsp kosher salt
⅛ tsp black pepper
¼ cup (31 g) all-purpose flour
½ tsp rosemary, finely chopped
1 cup (240 ml) red cooking wine
½ cup (160 g) fig jam
Zest of 1 orange
1 tbsp (8 g) cornstarch mixed with 1 tbsp (15 ml) cold water
4 cups (744 g) cooked jasmine rice, for serving

Turn the Instant Pot on to sauté mode. Add the butter to melt. Season the chicken with the salt and pepper. Dredge the seasoned chicken in the flour. Add the chicken to the pot and sauté in batches so as not to overcrowd the pot for 5 to 7 minutes, skin side down. Flip the chicken and add the rosemary and wine. Seal the lid and turn the valve to the sealing position. Turn the Instant Pot on manual, high pressure for 20 minutes. Manually release the pressure by carefully moving the valve to venting. Remove the chicken and shred. Remove 1 cup (240 ml) of the liquid and discard the rest. Return the chicken and the reserved liquid to the pot and add the fig jam, orange zest and cornstarch mixture. Serve the chicken over the rice.

RIBS

YIELD: 4 SERVINGS

The quickest way to make homemade, fall-off-the-bone ribs is in the Instant Pot. They come out perfectly every time. Make sure you remove the silver skin on the back of the ribs so they aren't chewy.

HONEY MUSTARD BBQ

KOREAN BBQ

ORANGE BBQ

MAPLE BBQ

HONEY MUSTARD BBQ RIBS

3 lbs (1.4 kg) rack baby back ribs
2 tbsp (24 g) smoky seasoning blend, such as McCormick Grill Mates Smokehouse Maple Seasoning
1 tsp liquid smoke

FOR THE SAUCE

½ cup (120 ml) yellow mustard
2 tbsp (30 ml) whole grain mustard
2 tbsp (30 ml) Worcestershire sauce
2 tbsp (30 ml) honey

Remove the silver skin from the back of the ribs. Season both sides with the seasoning blend and place the ribs on a rack in the Instant Pot (I bend them to stand them up and form a circle around the inside of the pot). Add 1 cup (240 ml) of water and liquid smoke to the bottom of the pot. Seal the lid and turn the valve to the sealing position. Turn the Instant Pot on manual, high pressure for 25 minutes. Let the pressure release naturally and then remove the ribs from the pot and place them on a foil-lined baking sheet.

Turn on the broiler. Combine the mustards, Worcestershire and honey in a small bowl. Liberally baste the ribs with half of the BBQ sauce and place them in the oven for 5 to 10 minutes, or until caramelized. Remove the ribs from the oven and baste again with the remaining sauce.

KOREAN BBQ RIBS

3 lbs (1.4 kg) rack baby back ribs
1 tbsp (7 g) Chinese five spice powder
1 tbsp (18 g) kosher salt

FOR THE SAUCE

¼ cup (60 ml) gochujang sauce
1 cup (240 ml) ketchup
1 tbsp (9 g) sesame seeds

Remove the silver skin from the back of the ribs. Season both sides with the Chinese five spice powder and salt and place them on a rack in the Instant Pot. I bend them to stand them up and form a circle around the inside of the pot. Add 1 cup (240 ml) of water to the bottom of the pot. Seal the lid and turn the valve to the sealing position. Turn the Instant Pot on manual, high pressure for 25 minutes. Let the pressure release naturally and then remove the ribs from the pot and place them on a foil-lined baking sheet.

Turn on the broiler. Combine the gochujang and ketchup in a small bowl. Liberally baste the ribs with half of the sauce and place them in the oven for 5 to 10 minutes, or until caramelized. Remove the ribs from the oven and baste again with the remaining sauce. Top with sesame seeds.

MAPLE BBQ RIBS

3 lbs (1.4 kg) rack baby back ribs
2 tbsp (24 g) smoky seasoning blend, such as McCormick Grill Mates Smokehouse Maple Seasoning
1 tsp liquid smoke

FOR THE SAUCE

1 cup (240 ml) BBQ sauce of your choice
¼ cup (60 ml) maple syrup

Remove the silver skin from the back of the ribs. Season both sides with the seasoning blend and place the ribs on a rack in the Instant Pot (I bend them to stand them up and form a circle around the inside of the pot). Add 1 cup (240 ml) of water and the liquid smoke to the bottom of the pot. Seal the lid and turn the valve to the sealing position. Turn the Instant Pot on manual, high pressure for 25 minutes. Let the pressure release naturally and then remove the ribs from the pot and place them on a foil-lined baking sheet.

Turn on the broiler. Combine the BBQ sauce and syrup in a small bowl. Liberally baste the ribs with half of the sauce and place them in the oven for 5 to 10 minutes, or until caramelized. Remove the ribs from the oven and baste again with the remaining sauce.

*See image on page 26.

ORANGE BBQ RIBS

3 lbs (1.4 kg) rack baby back ribs
2 tbsp (24 g) smoky seasoning blend, such as McCormick Grill Mates Smokehouse Maple Seasoning
1 tsp liquid smoke

FOR THE SAUCE

2 tsp orange zest (about 4 oranges)
½ cup (120 ml) orange juice
2 tsp (10 ml) honey
1 cup (240 ml) ketchup
½ tsp onion powder

Remove the silver skin from the back of the ribs. Season both sides with the seasoning blend and place the ribs on a rack in the Instant Pot (I bend them to stand them up and form a circle around the inside of the pot). Add 1 cup (240 ml) of water and the liquid smoke to the bottom of the pot. Seal the lid and turn the valve to the sealing position. Turn the Instant Pot on manual, high pressure for 25 minutes. Let the pressure release naturally and then remove the ribs from the pot and place them on a foil-lined baking sheet.

Turn on the broiler. Combine the orange zest and juice, honey, ketchup and onion powder in a small bowl. Liberally baste the ribs with half of the sauce and place them in the oven for 5 to 10 minutes, or until caramelized. Remove the ribs from the oven and baste again with the remaining sauce.

PORK SHOULDER

YIELD: 8 SERVINGS

Make sure you check out the Asian Pork Shoulder (page 32); it's my all-time favorite pork recipe. It's full of Asian flavors that go perfectly in tacos, with rice or stuffed in steamed bao buns. When cooking pork shoulder in the Instant Pot, I have found that cutting the pork shoulder into 2-inch (5-cm) strips helps reduce the cooking time significantly. You can buy pork shoulder that is already cut, labeled "pork shoulder country-style ribs." These are not actually ribs, just the shoulder cut into manageable strips.

CAFE RIO—STYLE

KALUA WITH PINEAPPLE
BBQ SAUCE

ASIAN

CITRUS CARNITAS

ASIAN PORK SHOULDER

1 tbsp (15 ml) avocado or olive oil

3 lbs (1.4 kg) country-style pork ribs or pork shoulder, cut into 2-inch (5-cm) chunks

2 tsp (12 g) kosher salt

2 tsp (10 ml) sesame oil

2 tsp (4 g) lemongrass, minced

2 tsp (4 g) minced fresh ginger

2 tsp (6 g) minced garlic, about 2 cloves

¼ cup (55 g) brown sugar

¼ cup (60 ml) fish sauce

½ cup (120 ml) hoisin sauce

FOR THE SLAW

½ cup (52 g) cucumber, julienned

½ cup (64 g) carrot, julienned

1 cup (240 ml) good quality pickle juice, such as Grillo's brand

Turn the Instant Pot on to sauté mode. Add the oil to the pot. Season the pork with the salt and sear on both sides in small batches so as to not overcrowd the pot. Add ½ cup (120 ml) of water, seal the lid and turn the valve to the sealing position. Turn the Instant Pot on manual, high pressure for 60 minutes. Let the pressure release naturally for 10 minutes. Remove the pork and dice it into small pieces.

Remove the excess liquid from the pot and discard. Add the sesame oil, lemongrass, ginger, garlic, brown sugar, fish sauce and hoisin, stirring to combine. Turn the Instant Pot on to sauté mode, add the pork back into the insert and simmer for 5 minutes. Prepare the slaw ingredients and let sit for at least 5 minutes. Serve the pork in tacos or on top of rice with slaw.

See image on page 30.

KALUA PORK SHOULDER WITH PINEAPPLE BBQ SAUCE

1 tbsp (15 ml) avocado or olive oil

3 lbs (1.4 kg) country-style pork ribs or pork shoulder, cut into 2-inch (5-cm) chunks

1 tbsp plus 2 tsp (30 g) kosher salt, divided

1 tbsp (15 ml) liquid smoke

1 cup (240 ml) ketchup

½ cup (120 ml) pineapple juice

½ tsp garlic powder

½ tsp chili powder

Coconut Rice (page 195), for serving

Turn the Instant Pot on to sauté mode. Add the oil to the pot. Season the pork with 2 teaspoons (12 g) of the salt and sear on both sides in small batches so as to not overcrowd the pot. Add the liquid smoke and 1 cup (240 ml) of water. Seal the lid and turn the valve to the sealing position. Turn the Instant Pot on manual, high pressure for 60 minutes. Let the pressure release naturally for 10 minutes.

Remove the excess liquid from the pot. Add the remaining 1 tablespoon (18 g) of salt, ketchup, pineapple juice, garlic powder and chili powder, stirring to combine. Turn the Instant Pot on to sauté mode and simmer for 5 minutes. Serve with Coconut Rice (page 195).

CITRUS CARNITAS PORK SHOULDER

1 tbsp (15 ml) avocado or olive oil

3 lbs (1.4 kg) country-style pork ribs or pork shoulder, cut into 2-inch (5-cm) chunks

5 tsp (30 g) kosher salt, divided

2 tbsp (18 g) minced garlic, about 5–6 cloves

1 white onion, sliced thinly (about 100 g)

2 tsp (6 g) chipotle chili in adobo, roughly chopped

2 tsp (4 g) lime zest

1 tsp orange zest

1 tsp garlic salt

½ tsp ground cumin

2 tsp (4 g) dried oregano

1 tsp onion powder

½ cup (120 ml) chicken stock

Maldon salt or finishing salt

Juice of 1 lime, about 2 tbsp (30 ml)

Warmed corn tortillas, for serving (optional)

Chopped cilantro, for serving (optional)

Diced white onion, for serving (optional)

Turn the Instant Pot on to sauté mode. Add the oil to the pot. Season the pork with 2 teaspoons (12 g) of the salt and sear on both sides in small batches so as to not overcrowd the pot. Remove the pork and then add the garlic and onion. Sauté for 1 to 2 minutes.

Add the chipotle, lime and orange zest, remaining 3 teaspoons (18 g) of the salt, garlic salt, cumin, oregano and onion powder. Add the pork back in along with the stock. Seal the lid and turn the valve to the sealing position. Turn the Instant Pot on manual, high pressure for 60 minutes. Let the pressure release naturally for 10 minutes. Remove the pork from the pot and shred with two forks.

Place the pork on a cookie sheet and spread it out in one even layer. Place the pork under the broiler for 5 to 7 minutes to caramelize. When the carnitas are done, season with coarse finishing salt and a squeeze of lime juice. Serve in tortillas with your toppings of choice.

CAFE RIO-STYLE PORK SHOULDER

1 tbsp (15 ml) avocado or olive oil

3 lbs (1.4 kg) country-style pork ribs or pork shoulder, cut into 2-inch (5-cm) chunks

4 tsp (24 g) kosher salt, divided

1 (12-oz [355-ml]) can Dr. Pepper or Coke

1 (28-oz [794-g]) can red enchilada sauce

¾ cup (165 g) brown sugar

Turn the Instant Pot on to sauté mode. Add the oil to the pot. Season the pork with 2 teaspoons (12 g) of the salt and sear on both sides in small batches so as to not overcrowd the pot. Add all the pork back into the insert along with the Dr. Pepper. Seal the lid and turn the valve to the sealing position. Turn the Instant Pot on manual, high pressure for 60 minutes. Let the pressure release naturally for 10 minutes.

Remove the excess liquid from the pot. Shred the pork and add the enchilada sauce, brown sugar and remaining 2 teaspoons (12 g) of salt and stir to combine. Turn the Instant Pot on to sauté mode and simmer for 5 minutes. Serve in burritos, on top of taco salad or in tacos.

MEATLOAF

YIELD: 4 SERVINGS

If you have ever had an overcooked, dried-out meatloaf, you have to try making meatloaf in the Instant Pot! My family loves meatloaf, especially the Loaded Burger Meatloaf (page 37). It's full of all of the typical burger flavors and can feed a family quickly.

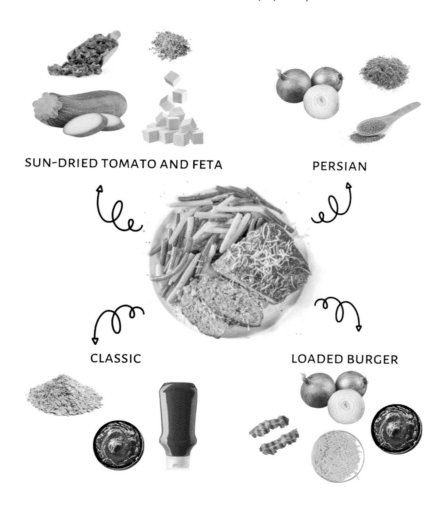

SUN-DRIED TOMATO AND FETA

PERSIAN

CLASSIC

LOADED BURGER

SUN-DRIED TOMATO AND FETA MEATLOAF

1 lb (454 g) ground turkey
¼ cup (14 g) sun-dried tomatoes, chopped fine
½ cup (62 g) zucchini, finely shredded
¼ cup (38 g) feta cheese
1 tsp Italian seasoning or herbs de Provence
½ cup (120 ml) ketchup, plus more for serving

In a mixing bowl combine the turkey, tomatoes, zucchini, feta cheese and dried herbs. Mix to combine. Place the meat mixture in a cake pan that fits your Instant Pot and pat down slightly to fill the pan. Top with the ketchup and cover with foil.

Add 1 cup (240 ml) of water to the insert and then add the trivet. Place the cake pan on the trivet and close the lid. Move the valve to sealing and cook on manual, high pressure for 50 minutes. Manually release the pressure by carefully moving the valve to venting. There will be excess liquid in the cake pan. Drain slightly and cut into wedges. Serve with extra ketchup.

*See image on page 34.

CLASSIC MEATLOAF

2 lbs (907 g) ground beef
½ cup (45 g) rolled oats
¾ cup (180 ml) ketchup
½ tsp kosher salt
1 tbsp (15 ml) Worcestershire sauce
½ cup (120 ml) BBQ sauce of choice, plus more for serving

In a mixing bowl combine the beef, oats, ketchup, salt and Worcestershire sauce. Mix to combine. Place the meat mixture in a cake pan that fits your Instant Pot and pat down slightly to fill the pan. Top with the BBQ sauce and cover with foil.

Add 1 cup (240 ml) of water to the insert and then add the trivet. Place the cake pan on the trivet and close the lid. Move the valve to sealing and cook on manual, high pressure for 50 minutes. Manually release the pressure by carefully moving the valve to venting. There will be excess liquid in the cake pan. Drain slightly and cut into wedges. Serve with extra BBQ sauce.

LOADED BURGER MEATLOAF

½ cup (80 g) white onion, diced
1 tbsp (14 g) unsalted butter
2 lbs (907 g) lean ground beef
1 cup (113 g) shredded cheddar cheese
½ cup (120 ml) BBQ sauce, plus extra for topping and serving
2 tsp (6 g) Montreal Steak Seasoning
4 slices of bacon, cooked until crispy and roughly chopped (about ¼ cup)

Turn the Instant Pot on to sauté mode. Add the onion and butter and sauté for 10 to 15 minutes to caramelize. Remove to a mixing bowl. Add the beef, cheddar cheese, BBQ sauce, Montreal seasoning and bacon and mix to combine. Place the meat mixture in a cake pan that fits your Instant Pot and pat down slightly to fill the pan. Top with extra BBQ sauce and cover with foil.

Add 1 cup (240 ml) of water to the insert and then add the trivet. Place the cake pan on the trivet and close the lid. Move the valve to sealing and cook on manual, high pressure for 50 minutes. Manually release the pressure by carefully moving the valve to venting. There will be excess liquid in the cake pan. Drain slightly and cut into wedges. Serve with extra BBQ sauce.

PERSIAN MEATLOAF

2 lbs (907 g) ground beef or lamb
2 tbsp (30 g) white onion, grated
1 tsp ground cumin
1 tsp ground coriander
1 tsp celery seed
1 tsp kosher salt

Combine all of the ingredients in a mixing bowl. Place the meat mixture in a cake pan that fits your size Instant Pot and pat down slightly to fill the pan. Cover with foil.

Add 1 cup (240 ml) of water to the insert and then add the trivet. Place the cake pan on the trivet and close the lid. Move the valve to sealing and cook on manual, high pressure for 50 minutes. Manually release the pressure by carefully moving the valve to venting. There will be excess liquid in the cake pan. Drain slightly and cut into wedges.

PASTA SHELLS

YIELD: 4 SERVINGS

There is nothing better than dumping ingredients into the Instant Pot and then having a delicious family-friendly dinner on hand in minutes. Shells in the Instant Pot only take two minutes and are perfect little vessels to scoop up the delicious sauces. I like to use a medium shell, but you can certainly use a small or large shell as well.

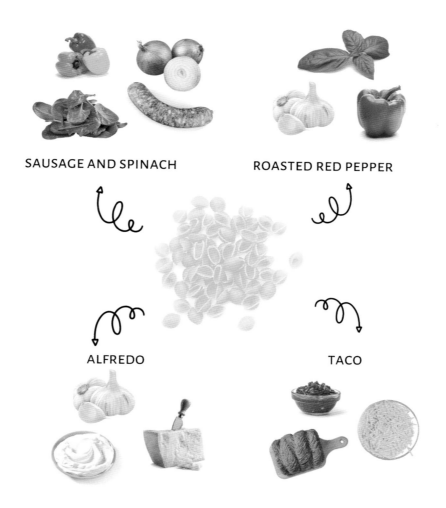

SAUSAGE AND SPINACH

ROASTED RED PEPPER

ALFREDO

TACO

SAUSAGE AND SPINACH SHELLS

2 tbsp (28 g) unsalted butter
1 lb (454 g) Italian chicken sausage
½ cup (80 g) white onion, diced small
1 cup (149 g) bell pepper (red or yellow), diced small
1 lb (454 g) medium shell pasta
5 cups (1.2 L) chicken stock
4 oz (113 g) cream cheese
4 cups (448 g) shredded Italian five cheese blend
1 cup frozen spinach, thawed and squeezed dry
Kosher salt and pepper, to taste

Turn the Instant Pot on to sauté mode. Add the butter to melt. Remove the sausage from the casing and brown in the Instant Pot. Break the sausage up into small pieces while browning. When it is almost cooked through, about 10 minutes, add the onion and pepper and cook for 2 minutes. Then add the shells and stock, seal the lid and turn the valve to the sealing position. Turn the Instant Pot on manual, high pressure for 2 minutes. Release the pressure manually by carefully moving the valve to venting.

Stir in the cream cheese, cheese blend and spinach until the cheese is melted completely. Taste for seasoning and adjust as needed with salt and pepper.

See image on page 38.

ROASTED RED PEPPER SHELLS

2 cloves garlic, minced
1 lb (454 g) medium shell pasta
4 tbsp (57 g) unsalted butter
5 cups (1.2 L) chicken stock
½ cup (92 g) jarred roasted red peppers, drained
¼ cup (6 g) basil leaves
4 oz (113 g) cream cheese, diced
8 oz (226 g) Italian-style blend shredded cheese
6 oz (170 g) Parmesan cheese, shredded
Kosher salt and pepper, to taste

Add the garlic, shells, butter and stock to the Instant Pot insert. Seal the lid and turn the valve to the sealing position. Turn the Instant Pot on manual, high pressure for 2 minutes. Release the pressure manually by carefully moving the valve to venting. Meanwhile, blend the roasted peppers and basil in a food processor until smooth and add it to the pot.

Stir in the cream cheese and shredded cheeses until melted completely. Taste for seasoning and add salt and pepper to taste.

TACO SHELLS

1 lb (454 g) ground beef
2 cups (480 ml) chicken stock
1 (28-oz [792-g]) can diced tomatoes, drained
2 tsp (7 g) taco seasoning
1 lb (454 g) medium shell pasta
1½ cups (360 ml) jarred red salsa
1 cup (113 g) shredded cheddar cheese
Diced avocado, for serving (optional)
Shredded cheddar cheese, for serving (optional)
Sour cream, for serving (optional)

Turn the Instant Pot on to sauté mode. Brown the ground beef, breaking it up with a spatula until the meat is cooked and browned, about 10 minutes. Add the stock, tomatoes, taco seasoning, shells and salsa in that order. Do not stir. Seal the lid and turn the valve to the sealing position. Turn the Instant Pot on manual, high pressure for 2 minutes. Release the pressure manually by carefully moving the valve to venting.

Stir in the cheddar cheese. Top with the desired toppings.

ALFREDO SHELLS

2 cloves garlic, minced
1 lb (454 g) medium shell pasta
4 tbsp (57 g) unsalted butter
5 cups (1.2 L) chicken stock
4 oz (113 g) cream cheese, diced
8 oz (226 g) Italian-style blend shredded cheese
6 oz (170 g) Parmesan cheese, shredded
Kosher salt and pepper, to taste

Add the garlic, shells, butter and stock to the Instant Pot insert. Seal the lid and turn the valve to the sealing position. Turn the Instant Pot on manual, high pressure for 2 minutes. Release the pressure manually by carefully moving the valve to venting.

Stir in the cream cheese and shredded cheeses until melted completely. Add salt and pepper to taste.

SPAGHETTI

Spaghetti is always a family favorite. I love being able to have a
one-pot dish for busy weeknights where I really don't have that much time to
cook. The classic Spaghetti with Meat Sauce (page 44) cooks up in about
8 minutes and can feed a crowd.

THAI CHICKEN

MEAT SAUCE

PUTTANESCA

CHICKEN PICCATA

THAI CHICKEN SPAGHETTI

1 cup (125 g) rotisserie chicken, shredded
2 carrots, peeled, julienned
8 oz (226 g) dry spaghetti pasta
2 cups (480 ml) water
½ cup (120 ml) peanut satay sauce
1 cup (112 g) shredded Italian five cheese blend

Add the chicken and carrots to the Instant Pot. Break the spaghetti in half and add it to the pot. Top with the water and peanut sauce. Do not stir. Seal the lid and turn the valve to the sealing position. Turn the Instant Pot on manual, high pressure for 8 minutes. Release the pressure manually by carefully moving the valve to venting. Stir in the cheese blend to melt.

SPAGHETTI WITH MEAT SAUCE

1 lb (454 g) ground beef
1 lb (454 g) Italian chicken sausage
3 cloves garlic, minced
1 cup (240 ml) red wine
8 oz (226 g) dry spaghetti pasta
2 cups (480 ml) water
24 oz (679 g) marinara sauce
Grated Parmesan cheese, for serving
5 basil leaves, sliced into chiffonade (see Note), for serving

Turn the Instant Pot on to sauté mode. Brown the beef and sausage, breaking it up with a spatula until the meat is cooked and browned, about 10 minutes. Add the garlic and wine and scrape any bits from the bottom of the pot. Break the spaghetti in half and add it to the pot. Top with the water and marinara sauce. Do not stir. Seal the lid and turn the valve to the sealing position.

Turn the Instant Pot on manual, high pressure for 8 minutes. Release the pressure manually by carefully moving the valve to venting. Stir to combine. Serve with the Parmesan and basil.

NOTE

To chiffonade basil, stack the basil leaves on top of each other and roll tightly like a cigar. Slice the basil roll into thin, ⅛-inch (3-mm) slices by moving your knife back and forth in a rocking motion. Make sure your basil is completely dry to prevent bruising.

CHICKEN PICCATA SPAGHETTI

1 lb (454 g) boneless, skinless chicken breasts, cut in half lengthwise
1 cup (56 g) panko bread crumbs
4 tbsp (57 g) unsalted butter, cubed
Kosher salt and pepper, to taste
2 cloves garlic, minced
1 cup (240 ml) white cooking wine
8 oz (226 g) dry spaghetti pasta
2 cups (480 ml) chicken stock
1 tbsp (7 g) capers
Zest of 1 lemon
Shredded Parmesan cheese, for serving (optional)

Turn the Instant Pot on to sauté mode. Dredge the chicken in the bread crumbs, pressing down to coat. Add the butter to the pot and sauté the chicken breasts for 5 to 7 minutes per side, or until cooked and golden brown. Try not to move the chicken too much. Remove the chicken from the Instant Pot, season with salt and pepper and set aside. Add the garlic and wine to the pot and scrape any bits from the bottom of the pot. Break the spaghetti in half and add it to the pot. Top with the stock. Do not stir. Seal the lid and turn the valve to the sealing position.

Turn the Instant Pot on manual, high pressure for 8 minutes. Release the pressure manually by carefully moving the valve to venting. Stir in the capers and lemon zest. Slice the chicken into bite-sized pieces. Serve the chicken on top of the spaghetti and top with the Parmesan, if using.

See image on page 42.

PUTTANESCA SPAGHETTI

1 tbsp (15 ml) olive oil
2 cloves garlic, minced
8 oz (226 g) dry spaghetti pasta
2 cups (480 ml) water
1 (14.5-oz [411-g]) can diced tomatoes, drained
¼ cup (32 g) kalamata olives, pitted and sliced
1 tbsp (7 g) capers
⅛ tsp red pepper flakes
¼ cup (25 g) Parmesan cheese, grated
1 tsp parsley, finely chopped

Turn the Instant Pot on to sauté mode. Add the oil and garlic and sauté for 3 minutes. Break the spaghetti in half and add it to the pot. Top with the water. Do not stir. Seal the lid and turn the valve to the sealing position.

Turn the Instant Pot on manual, high pressure for 8 minutes. Release the pressure manually by carefully moving the valve to venting. Stir in the tomatoes, olives, capers and red pepper flakes. Top with the Parmesan and parsley.

MAC AND CHEESE

YIELD: 8 SERVINGS

It only takes one time making this recipe and you will never want to go back to the box stuff. Kid-approved and full of flavor, all of these macaroni combinations are perfect for a quick family dinner.

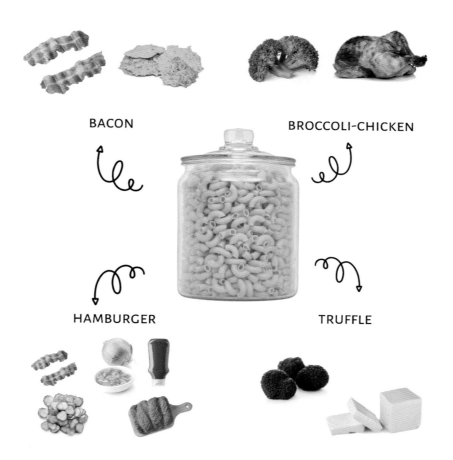

BACON

BROCCOLI-CHICKEN

HAMBURGER

TRUFFLE

BACON MAC AND CHEESE

5 slices applewood smoked bacon
1 (16-oz [454-g]) bag large elbow macaroni noodles
4 tbsp (57 g) unsalted butter
5 cups (1.2 L) chicken stock
4 oz (113 g) cream cheese, diced
6 cups (678 g) shredded cheddar cheese
2 tsp (12 g) kosher salt
1 cup (56 g) panko bread crumbs or cheese crackers, broken into small pieces

Turn the Instant Pot on to sauté mode. Cook the bacon until crispy, about 10 minutes, roughly chop, then set aside. Clean out the insert. Place the macaroni, butter and stock in the Instant Pot insert. Seal the lid and turn the valve to the sealing position. Turn the Instant Pot on manual, high pressure for 3 minutes. Release the pressure manually by carefully moving the valve to venting.

Add the cream cheese, cheddar cheese, bacon and salt, stirring until the cheese is melted. Transfer to a foil baking dish and top with the panko bread crumbs. Turn the broiler on to low. When the oven is ready, place the pan under the broiler for 3 minutes, or until the top is golden.

BROCCOLI-CHICKEN MAC AND CHEESE

1 (16-oz [454-g]) bag large elbow macaroni noodles
4 tbsp (57 g) unsalted butter
5 cups (1.2 L) chicken stock
4 oz (113 g) cream cheese, diced
6 cups (678 g) shredded cheddar cheese
1 cup (125 g) rotisserie chicken, shredded
1 cup (87 g) frozen broccoli, defrosted and roughly chopped
2 tsp (12 g) kosher salt
1 cup (56 g) panko bread crumbs or cheese crackers, broken into small pieces

Place the macaroni, butter and stock in the Instant Pot insert. Seal the lid and turn the valve to the sealing position. Turn the Instant Pot on manual, high pressure for 3 minutes. Release the pressure manually by carefully moving the valve to venting.

Add the cream cheese, cheddar cheese, chicken, broccoli and salt, stirring until the cheese is melted. Transfer to a foil baking dish and top with the panko bread crumbs. Turn the broiler on to low. When the oven is ready, place the pan under the broiler for 3 minutes, or until the top is golden.

See image on page 46.

HAMBURGER MAC AND CHEESE

1 lb (454 g) ground beef
1 (16-oz [454-g]) bag large elbow macaroni noodles
2 tbsp (28 g) unsalted butter
5 cups (1.2 L) chicken stock
4 oz (113 g) cream cheese, diced
6 cups (678 g) shredded cheddar cheese
2 tsp (6 g) Montreal Steak Seasoning
1 cup (56 g) panko bread crumbs or bread crumbs
Diced pickles, for topping
Crispy bacon, for topping
Ketchup, for topping
Caramelized onions, for topping

Turn the Instant Pot on to sauté mode. Add the ground beef and brown, breaking the meat into small pieces until cooked through, about 10 minutes. Remove and set aside. Clean out the insert. Add the macaroni, butter and stock. Seal the lid and turn the valve to the sealing position. Turn the Instant Pot on manual, high pressure for 3 minutes. Release the pressure manually by carefully moving the valve to venting.

Add the cooked meat, cream cheese, cheddar cheese and Montreal seasoning and stir until the cheese is melted. Transfer to a foil baking dish and top with the panko bread crumbs. Turn the broiler on to low. When the oven is ready, place the pan under the broiler for 3 minutes, or until the top is golden. Top individual servings with your toppings of choice.

TRUFFLE MAC AND CHEESE

1 (16-oz [454-g]) bag large elbow macaroni noodles
4 tbsp (60 g) truffle butter
6 cups (1.4 L) chicken stock
4 oz (113 g) cream cheese, diced
6 cups (672 g) shredded Italian five cheese blend
2 tsp (12 g) kosher salt
1 cup (56 g) panko bread crumbs or cheese crackers, broken into small pieces

Place the macaroni, truffle butter and stock in the Instant Pot insert. Seal the lid and turn the valve to the sealing position. Turn the Instant Pot on manual, high pressure for 3 minutes. Release the pressure manually by carefully moving the valve to venting.

Add the cream cheese, shredded cheese and salt, stirring until the cheese is melted. Transfer to a foil baking dish and top with panko bread crumbs. Turn the broiler on to low. When the oven is ready, place the pan under the broiler for 3 minutes, or until the top is golden.

RISOTTO

What would normally take over 30 minutes on the stovetop stirring constantly, only takes 10 minutes in the Instant Pot. My favorite Butternut Squash Risotto (page 52) proves you don't have to slave over the stove to create this rich, creamy, Italian rice dish.

BUTTERNUT SQUASH

PESTO-SHRIMP

TOMATO-BASIL

MUSHROOM

BUTTERNUT SQUASH RISOTTO

FOR THE BUTTERNUT SQUASH TOPPING

2 tbsp (28 g) unsalted butter

1 lb (454 g) butternut squash, peeled, ends removed and diced

1 tbsp (15 ml) maple syrup

1 tsp fresh sage, finely chopped

½ tsp kosher salt

FOR THE BASE RISOTTO

1 tbsp (14 g) unsalted butter

1 shallot, minced

2 cups (394 g) arborio rice

¼ cup (60 ml) white cooking wine or white wine

4 cups (960 ml) chicken stock

½ cup (50 g) Parmesan cheese, grated, plus more for garnish

1 tbsp (14 g) garlic butter or unsalted butter

½ tsp kosher salt

Turn the Instant Pot on to sauté mode. Add the butter and squash and sauté for 10 minutes stirring occasionally. Add the syrup, sage and salt and stir to combine. Remove the squash mixture and place it in a bowl. Cover with plastic wrap and let it steam while you prepare the risotto.

Clean out the insert. Turn the Instant Pot on to sauté mode. Add the butter and shallot and sauté for 1 to 2 minutes to soften. Add the rice and sauté for 2 minutes, making sure you stir to coat the rice in the butter. Add the wine and stir to release any rice from the bottom of the pot. Add the stock. Place the lid on the pot and turn the valve to sealing. Cook on manual, high pressure for 5 minutes. Manually release the pressure by carefully moving the valve to venting. Stir in the cheese, butter and salt.

Top the risotto with the squash and sprinkle with more Parmesan cheese.

PESTO-SHRIMP RISOTTO

FOR THE PESTO-SHRIMP TOPPING

1 tbsp (14 g) unsalted butter

1 lb (454 g) raw shrimp, peeled and deveined

½ cup (115 g) pesto

FOR THE BASE RISOTTO

1 tbsp (14 g) unsalted butter

1 shallot, minced

2 cups (394 g) arborio rice

¼ cup (60 ml) white cooking wine or white wine

4 cups (960 ml) chicken stock

½ cup (50 g) Parmesan cheese, grated, plus more for garnish

1 tbsp (14 g) garlic butter or unsalted butter

½ tsp kosher salt

Turn the Instant Pot on to sauté mode. Add the butter and shrimp and sauté for 5 minutes, stirring occasionally until the shrimp are pink. Remove the shrimp and place in a bowl. Toss with the pesto.

Clean out the insert. Turn the Instant Pot on to sauté mode. Add the butter and shallot and sauté for 1 to 2 minutes to soften. Add the rice and sauté for 2 minutes, making sure you stir to coat the rice in the butter. Add the cooking wine and stir to release any rice from the bottom of the pot. Add the stock. Place the lid on the pot and turn the valve to sealing. Cook on manual, high pressure for 5 minutes. Manually release the pressure by carefully moving the valve to venting. Stir in the Parmesan, butter and salt.

Top the risotto with the shrimp mixture and sprinkle with more Parmesan cheese.

See image on page 50.

TOMATO-BASIL RISOTTO

FOR THE TOMATO-BASIL TOPPING

3 cups (540 g) heirloom tomatoes, diced

2 cloves garlic, minced

5 basil leaves, sliced into chiffonade (see Note on page 44)

1 tbsp (15 ml) extra-virgin olive oil

½ tsp coarse salt

FOR THE BASE RISOTTO

1 tbsp (14 g) unsalted butter

1 shallot, minced

2 cups (394 g) arborio rice

¼ cup (60 ml) white cooking wine or white wine

4 cups (960 ml) chicken stock

½ cup (50 g) Parmesan cheese, grated

1 tbsp (14 g) garlic butter or unsalted butter

½ tsp kosher salt

Balsamic glaze, for garnish

In a medium bowl, combine the tomatoes, garlic, basil, oil and coarse salt and let sit for 5 minutes.

Turn the Instant Pot on to sauté mode. Add the butter and shallot and sauté for 1 to 2 minutes to soften. Add the rice and sauté for 2 minutes, making sure you stir to coat the rice in the butter. Add the wine and stir to release any rice from the bottom of the pot. Add the stock. Place the lid on the pot and turn the valve to sealing. Cook on manual, high pressure for 5 minutes. Manually release the pressure by carefully moving the valve to venting. Stir in the Parmesan, butter and salt.

Top the risotto with the bruschetta and drizzle with balsamic glaze.

MUSHROOM RISOTTO

FOR THE MUSHROOM TOPPING

2 tbsp (28 g) unsalted butter

1 lb (454 g) button mushrooms, thinly sliced

2 cloves garlic, minced

1 tsp fresh thyme leaves, stripped from the sprigs and roughly chopped

½ cup (120 ml) white wine

FOR THE BASE RISOTTO

1 tbsp (14 g) unsalted butter

1 shallot, minced

2 cups (394 g) arborio rice

¼ cup (60 ml) white cooking wine or white wine

4 cups (960 ml) chicken stock

½ cup (50 g) Parmesan cheese, grated, plus more for garnish

1 tbsp (14 g) garlic butter or unsalted butter

½ tsp kosher salt

Turn the Instant Pot on to sauté mode. Add the butter, mushrooms, garlic and thyme and sauté for 5 to 7 minutes or until brown. Deglaze the pot with the wine and simmer for 5 minutes. Remove the mushroom topping from the pot and set aside.

Clean out the insert. Turn the Instant Pot on to sauté mode. Add the butter and shallot and sauté for 1 to 2 minutes to soften. Add the rice and sauté for 2 minutes, making sure you stir to coat the rice in the butter. Add the cooking wine and stir to release any rice from the bottom of the pot. Add the stock. Place the lid on the pot and turn the valve to sealing. Cook on manual, high pressure for 5 minutes. Manually release the pressure by carefully moving the valve to venting. Stir in the Parmesan, butter and salt.

Serve the mushrooms on top of the risotto and top with more Parmesan.

BAKED POTATO

YIELD: 4 SERVINGS

I love baked potatoes for a quick and easy dinner for the family. Stuff them with these delicious varieties or have a baked potato bar with a few of your family's favorite toppings for another quick dinner idea. Potatoes are one of those items that can cook differently depending on the size. For large potatoes, cook for around 30 minutes. For smaller potatoes, cook for 20 minutes.

TACO CAULIFLOWER

GREEK CHICKEN

CHICKEN CURRY

STEAK AND BLUE CHEESE

STEAK AND BLUE CHEESE BAKED POTATO

4 large Russet potatoes, rinsed and poked with a fork around the entire surface

FOR THE STEAK AND BLUE CHEESE FILLING

2 tbsp (28 g) unsalted butter

1½ lbs (680 g) beef stew meat

Kosher salt and pepper, to taste

2 tbsp (16 g) all-purpose flour

1 cup (240 ml) beef stock

4 oz (113 g) crumbled blue cheese

½ cup (120 ml) heavy cream

Add 1 cup (240 ml) of water to the Instant Pot insert. With a trivet on the bottom, place the potatoes inside. Seal with the lid and turn the valve to the sealing position. Cook on manual, high pressure for 30 minutes. Let the pressure release naturally for 10 minutes. Remove the potatoes from the Instant Pot. Wrap the potatoes in foil or place them in an oven preheated to 200°F (93°C) to keep them warm while you make the filling.

Clean out the insert. Turn the Instant Pot on to sauté mode and add the butter. Pat the meat down with a paper towel and season with salt and pepper. Sear in batches so as not to overcrowd the pot for 5 to 7 minutes until browned. Add the flour and stir to combine. Add the stock, seal the lid and turn the valve to the sealing position. Cook on manual, high pressure for 30 minutes. Release the pressure manually by carefully moving the valve to venting. Stir in the blue cheese and cream. Serve in the potatoes.

*See image on page 54.

TACO CAULIFLOWER BAKED POTATO

4 large Russet potatoes, rinsed and poked with a fork around the entire surface

FOR THE TACO FILLING

1 tsp avocado or olive oil

1 large head of cauliflower, cut into roughly ¼-inch (6-mm) pieces

1 tsp chili powder

1 tsp garlic salt

½ tsp dried oregano

¼ tsp ground cumin

½–1 cup (120–240 ml) red salsa, to taste

Shredded cheddar cheese, for topping

Diced avocado, for topping

Salsa, for topping

Sour cream, for topping

Add 1 cup (240 ml) of water to the Instant Pot insert. With a trivet on the bottom, place the potatoes inside. Seal with the lid and turn the valve to the sealing position. Cook on manual, high pressure for 30 minutes. Let the pressure release naturally for 10 minutes. Remove the potatoes from the Instant Pot.

Clean out the insert. Turn the Instant Pot on to sauté mode. Add the oil and cauliflower and sauté for 5 minutes, stirring occasionally. Add the chili powder, garlic salt, oregano, cumin and salsa and cook for another 5 minutes, stirring occasionally. Serve the cauliflower in the potatoes and add your toppings of choice.

GREEK CHICKEN BAKED POTATO

4 large Russet potatoes, rinsed and poked with a fork around the entire surface

FOR THE GREEK CHICKEN FILLING

1 lb (454 g) boneless, skinless chicken breast
1 (12-oz [340-g]) jar pepperoncini
1 (0.7-oz [19-g]) packet dry Italian dressing mix
Crumbled feta cheese, for topping
Sliced kalamata olives, for topping

Add 1 cup (240 ml) of water to the Instant Pot insert. With a trivet on the bottom, place the potatoes inside. Seal with the lid and turn the valve to the sealing position. Cook on manual, high pressure for 30 minutes. Let the pressure release naturally for 10 minutes. Remove the potatoes from the Instant Pot. Wrap the potatoes in foil or place them in an oven preheated to 200°F (93°C) to keep them warm while you make the filling.

Clean out the insert. Add the chicken, pepperoncini and liquid from the jar and Italian dressing mix. Seal the lid and turn the valve to the sealing position. Cook on manual, high pressure for 17 minutes. Release the pressure manually by carefully moving the valve to venting. Shred the chicken with two forks. Serve the chicken in the potatoes and add your toppings of choice.

CHICKEN CURRY BAKED POTATO

4 large Russet potatoes, rinsed and poked with a fork around the entire surface

FOR THE CHICKEN CURRY FILLING

1 tbsp (15 ml) avocado or olive oil
1½ lbs (680 g) boneless, skinless chicken breasts, cut into 1-inch (3-cm) slices
1 (13.5-oz [383-g]) can of coconut milk
1 tsp kosher salt, plus more to taste
2 tsp (8 g) brown sugar
2 tsp (4 g) curry powder
Zest of 1 lime

Add 1 cup (240 ml) of water to the Instant Pot insert. With a trivet on the bottom, place the potatoes inside. Seal with the lid and turn the valve to the sealing position. Cook on manual, high pressure for 30 minutes. Let the pressure release naturally for 10 minutes. Remove the potatoes from the Instant Pot.

Clean out the insert. Turn the Instant Pot on to sauté mode. Add the oil and chicken and sauté for 5 minutes. Add the coconut milk, salt, brown sugar and curry powder and seal with the lid. Turn the valve to the sealing position and cook on manual, high pressure for 2 minutes. Manually release the pressure by carefully moving the valve to venting. Stir in the lime zest and season with salt to taste. Top the potatoes with the chicken curry.

SPAGHETTI SQUASH

YIELD: 4 SERVINGS

Spaghetti squash is a great low carb option for a quick, healthy dinner. If you have trouble cutting your squash, poke holes with a knife around the entire surface and microwave it for 2 minutes to soften the skin slightly.

SHRIMP PAD THAI

TURKEY BURGER BOAT

CHICKEN TERIYAKI

TACO BOAT

CHICKEN TERIYAKI SPAGHETTI SQUASH

1 large spaghetti squash, cut in half lengthwise

FOR THE CHICKEN TERIYAKI TOPPING

1 tsp avocado or olive oil

2 lbs (907 g) boneless, skinless chicken breast, cut into ½-inch (1.3-cm) pieces

1 (16-oz [454-g]) bag fresh stir-fry vegetable mix

½ cup (120 ml) liquid aminos, such as Bragg Liquid Aminos

½ cup (120 ml) water

2 tsp (10 ml) sesame oil

2 tsp (4 g) grated fresh ginger

½ cup (100 g) brown sugar

1 tbsp (8 g) cornstarch mixed with 1 tbsp (15 ml) water

Add 1 cup (240 ml) of water to the Instant Pot. Place the spaghetti squash in a steamer basket and lower it into the pot. Seal the lid and turn the valve to the sealing position. Turn the Instant Pot on manual, high pressure for 7 minutes. Release the pressure manually by carefully moving the valve to venting. Remove the seeds and run a fork along the flesh of the squash to create strands. Set aside.

Clean out the insert. Turn the Instant Pot on to sauté mode. Add the oil and chicken and sauté for 7 minutes. Add the stir-fry mix and cook until the chicken is cooked through, about 3 more minutes. While the chicken is cooking, place the liquid aminos, water, sesame oil, ginger and brown sugar in a small saucepan and bring it to a simmer. Add the cornstarch mixture and stir to combine and thicken. Add the sauce to the chicken and stir to combine. Top the spaghetti squash with the chicken and vegetable mixture.

TACO BOAT SPAGHETTI SQUASH

1 large spaghetti squash, cut in half lengthwise

FOR THE TACO FILLING

1 lb (454 g) ground beef or ground turkey

1 tsp garlic salt

2 tsp (4 g) chili powder

1 tsp dry oregano

½ tsp ground cumin

½ cup (120 ml) red salsa

Shredded cheddar cheese, for topping

Diced avocado, for topping

Salsa, for topping

Add 1 cup (240 ml) of water to the Instant Pot. Place the spaghetti squash in a steamer basket and lower it into the pot. Seal the lid and turn the valve to the sealing position. Turn the Instant Pot on manual, high pressure for 7 minutes. Release the pressure manually by carefully moving the valve to venting. Remove the seeds and run a fork along the flesh of the squash to create strands. Set aside.

Clean out the insert. Turn the Instant Pot on to sauté mode. Sauté the ground beef until browned and cooked through, about 10 minutes. Remove any excess grease and add the garlic salt, chili powder, oregano, cumin and salsa to the beef. Cook for an additional 2 minutes. Stuff the spaghetti squash with the ground meat mixture and top with your toppings of choice.

TURKEY BURGER BOAT SPAGHETTI SQUASH

1 large spaghetti squash, cut in half lengthwise

FOR THE HAMBURGER FILLING

1 lb (454 g) ground turkey
1 tsp Montreal Steak Seasoning
½ cup (57 g) shredded cheddar cheese
4 slices applewood smoked bacon, cooked until crispy and roughly chopped
10 cherry tomatoes, cut in half
2 tbsp (18 g) pickle chips, cut in half
Ketchup, for topping
Mustard, for topping
Sesame seeds, for topping

Add 1 cup (240 ml) of water to the Instant Pot. Place the spaghetti squash in a steamer basket and lower it into the pot. Seal the lid and turn the valve to the sealing position. Turn the Instant Pot on manual, high pressure for 7 minutes. Release the pressure manually by carefully moving the valve to venting. Remove the seeds and run a fork along the flesh of the squash to create strands. Set aside.

Clean out the insert. Turn the Instant Pot on to sauté mode. Sauté the ground turkey with the steak seasoning until browned and cooked through, about 10 minutes. Remove and set aside. Stuff the spaghetti squash with the ground turkey mixture and top with the cheddar cheese. Place the squash under the broiler for 4 minutes to melt the cheese. Top with bacon, tomatoes, pickles, ketchup, mustard and sesame seeds.

SHRIMP PAD THAI SPAGHETTI SQUASH

1 large spaghetti squash, cut in half lengthwise

FOR THE PAD THAI FILLING

2 tsp (10 ml) oil
1 lb (454 g) peeled and deveined shrimp, tails removed
2 cloves garlic, minced
2 carrots, peeled and julienned
3 tbsp (42 g) brown sugar
2 tbsp (30 ml) fish sauce
3 tbsp (45 ml) liquid aminos, such as Bragg Liquid Aminos
1 tsp sesame oil
3 eggs, beaten
2 cups (200 g) bean sprouts
3 green onions, sliced thinly
2 limes, sliced into wedges
Cilantro, roughly chopped, for topping
Peanuts, roughly chopped, for topping

Add 1 cup (240 ml) of water to the Instant Pot. Place the spaghetti squash in a steamer basket and lower it into the pot. Seal the lid and turn the valve to the sealing position. Turn the Instant Pot on manual, high pressure for 7 minutes. Release the pressure manually by carefully moving the valve to venting. Remove the seeds and run a fork along the flesh of the squash to create strands. Strain any excess liquid from the squash. Set aside.

Clean out the insert. Turn the Instant Pot on to sauté mode. Add the oil, shrimp and garlic and sauté for 4 minutes. Add the carrots, brown sugar, fish sauce and liquid aminos and cook for 2 minutes. Remove the shrimp mixture and place it into a bowl. Add the sesame oil to the insert and scramble the eggs, about 3 minutes. Add the shrimp mixture back to the pot along with the bean sprouts, green onions and spaghetti squash. Cook for 2 to 4 minutes to combine. Squeeze the lime wedges over the mixture and top with cilantro and peanuts.

See image on page 58.

SOUPS AND STEWS

Nothing is better than warm soup on a cold day. The ultimate comfort food can be easily made in the Instant Pot with these soup recipes, each with four variations for you to try. I love that I can make one of these soups quickly and serve them straight from the pot. When our schedules get crazy busy and family members get home at different times, the soup is still warm and delicious.

CHICKEN NOODLE SOUP

YIELD: 6 SERVINGS

Nothing beats chicken noodle soup when you need a comforting meal.
I make double batches of this recipe and place them in storage
containers to freeze for when I really don't feel like cooking or
to take to sick neighbors and friends.

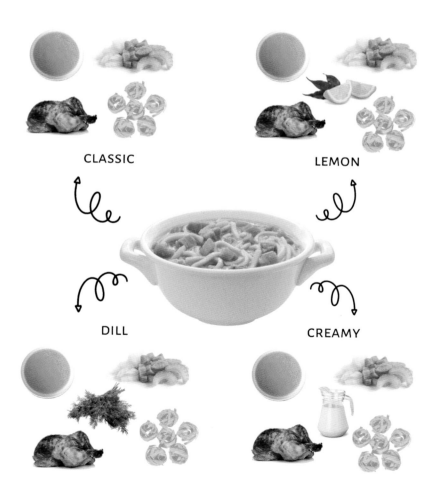

CLASSIC

LEMON

DILL

CREAMY

CLASSIC CHICKEN NOODLE SOUP

1 tbsp (14 g) unsalted butter

1 cup (160 g) white onion, diced small

2 cups (202 g) celery, diced small

2 cups (256 g) carrots, diced small

2 cups (250 g) rotisserie chicken, shredded

2 (32-oz [907-g]) containers chicken stock or bone broth

1 (8-oz [226-g]) bag pappardelle noodles or noodle of choice

1 tsp kosher salt

⅛ tsp black pepper

Turn the Instant Pot on to sauté mode. Add the butter and onion and sauté for 2 to 3 minutes. Add the celery and carrots and cook for 5 minutes, stirring occasionally. Add the chicken and stock and seal with the lid. Move the valve to the sealing position, and cook on manual, high pressure for 5 minutes. Turn the Instant Pot back on to sauté mode and add the noodles, salt and pepper. Cook for 5 to 7 minutes, or until the noodles are cooked through.

LEMON CHICKEN NOODLE SOUP

1 tbsp (14 g) unsalted butter

1 cup (160 g) white onion, diced small

2 cups (202 g) celery, diced small

2 cups (256 g) carrots, diced small

2 cups (250 g) rotisserie chicken, shredded

2 (32-oz [907-g]) containers chicken stock or bone broth

1 (8-oz [226-g]) bag pappardelle noodles or noodle of choice

1 tsp kosher salt

⅛ tsp black pepper

Zest of 2 lemons

Turn the Instant Pot on to sauté mode. Add the butter and onion and sauté for 2 to 3 minutes. Add the celery and carrots and cook for 5 minutes, stirring occasionally. Add the chicken and stock and seal with the lid. Move the valve to the sealing position and cook on manual, high pressure for 5 minutes. Turn the Instant Pot back on to sauté mode and add the noodles, salt and pepper. Cook for 5 to 7 minutes, or until the noodles are cooked through. Add the lemon zest and stir to combine.

DILL CHICKEN NOODLE SOUP

1 tbsp (14 g) unsalted butter
1 cup (160 g) white onion, diced small
2 cups (202 g) celery, diced small
2 cups (256 g) carrots, diced small
2 cups (250 g) rotisserie chicken, shredded
2 (32-oz [907-g]) containers chicken stock or bone broth
1 (8-oz [226-g]) bag pappardelle noodles or noodle of choice
1 tsp kosher salt
⅛ tsp black pepper
1 tbsp (3 g) fresh dill, roughly chopped

Turn the Instant Pot on to sauté mode. Add the butter and onion and sauté for 2 to 3 minutes. Add the celery and carrots and cook for 5 minutes, stirring occasionally. Add the chicken and stock and seal with the lid. Move the valve to the sealing position and cook on manual, high pressure for 5 minutes. Turn the Instant Pot back on to sauté mode and add the noodles, salt and pepper. Cook for 5 to 7 minutes, or until the noodles are cooked through. Add the dill and stir to combine.

CREAMY CHICKEN NOODLE SOUP

1 tbsp (14 g) unsalted butter
1 cup (160 g) white onion, diced small
2 cups (202 g) celery, diced small
2 cups (256 g) carrots, diced small
2 cups (250 g) rotisserie chicken, shredded
2 (32-oz [907-g]) containers chicken stock or bone broth
1 (8-oz [226-g]) bag pappardelle noodles or noodle of choice
1 tsp kosher salt
⅛ tsp black pepper
½ cup (120 ml) heavy cream
2 tbsp (16 g) cornstarch mixed with 2 tbsp (30 ml) cold water

Turn the Instant Pot on to sauté mode. Add the butter and onion and sauté for 2 to 3 minutes. Add the celery and carrots and cook for 5 minutes, stirring occasionally. Add the chicken and stock and seal with the lid. Move the valve to the sealing position and cook on manual, high pressure for 5 minutes. Turn the Instant Pot back on to sauté mode and add the noodles, salt and pepper. Cook for 5 to 7 minutes, or until the noodles are cooked through. Add the cream and cornstarch mixture and stir to combine. Cook for an additional 3 minutes to thicken.

See image on page 64.

BEEF STEW

YIELD: 4 SERVINGS

This recipe makes beef stew in half the time with beef that is tender and melts in your mouth. I love making the Guinness Beef Stew (page 70) on a cold winter night, and it's one of my go-to recipes to make for people who just moved into the neighborhood. It's simply comfort food at its finest.

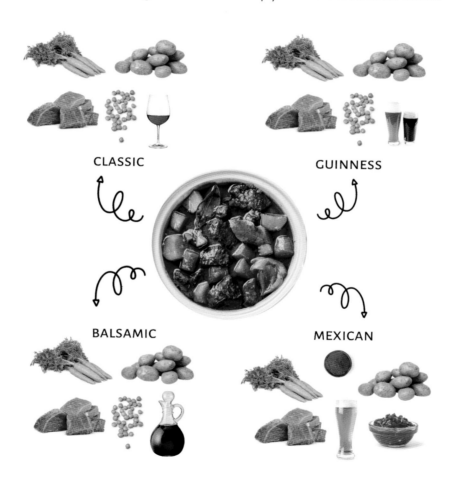

CLASSIC

GUINNESS

BALSAMIC

MEXICAN

CLASSIC BEEF STEW

1 lb (454 g) beef stew meat

Kosher salt and black pepper

1 tbsp (14 g) unsalted butter

2 cups (256 g) carrots, diced

2 cups (300 g) Russet potatoes, peeled, diced in 1-inch (3-cm) chunks

1 (1-oz [28-g]) packet onion soup mix

1 (14.5-oz [411-g]) can diced tomatoes, drained

1 cup (240 ml) red cooking wine

3 sprigs fresh thyme, leaves stripped

1 tbsp (8 g) cornstarch mixed with 2 tbsp (30 ml) water

½ cup (67 g) frozen peas

Turn the Instant Pot on to sauté mode. Pat the meat dry with a paper towel to remove any excess moisture, then season with salt and pepper on all sides. Add the butter to the Instant Pot insert and sear the meat, working in batches if necessary, until golden brown on all sides. Add the carrots, potatoes, soup mix, tomatoes, wine and thyme and stir to combine. Seal the lid and turn the valve to the sealing position. Turn the Instant Pot on manual, high pressure for 40 minutes. Release the pressure manually by carefully moving the valve to venting. Turn the Instant Pot on to sauté mode again and add the cornstarch mixture along with the frozen peas. Stir for 3 minutes until thickened.

See image on page 68.

GUINNESS BEEF STEW

1 lb (454 g) beef stew meat

Kosher salt and black pepper

1 tbsp (14 g) unsalted butter

2 cups (256 g) carrots, diced

2 cups (300 g) Russet potatoes, peeled, diced in 1-inch (3-cm) chunks

1 (1-oz [28-g]) packet onion soup mix

1 (14.5-oz [411-g]) can diced tomatoes, drained

1 cup (240 ml) Guinness

3 sprigs fresh thyme, leaves stripped

1 tbsp (8 g) cornstarch mixed with 2 tbsp (30 ml) water

½ cup (67 g) frozen peas

Turn the Instant Pot on to sauté mode. Pat the meat dry with a paper towel to remove any excess moisture, then season with salt and pepper on all sides. Add the butter to the Instant Pot insert and sear the meat, working in batches if necessary, until golden brown on all sides. Add the carrots, potatoes, soup mix, tomatoes, Guinness and thyme and stir to combine. Seal the lid and turn the valve to the sealing position. Turn the Instant Pot on manual, high pressure for 40 minutes. Release the pressure manually by carefully moving the valve to venting. Turn the Instant Pot on to sauté mode again and add the cornstarch mixture along with the frozen peas. Stir for 3 minutes until thickened.

BALSAMIC BEEF STEW

1 lb (454 g) beef stew meat

Kosher salt and black pepper

1 tbsp (14 g) unsalted butter

2 cups (256 g) carrots, diced

2 cups (300 g) Russet potatoes, peeled, diced in 1-inch (3-cm) chunks

1 (1-oz [28-g]) packet onion soup mix

1 (14.5-oz [411-g]) can diced tomatoes, drained

½ cup (120 ml) balsamic vinegar

3 sprigs fresh thyme

1 tbsp (8 g) cornstarch mixed with 2 tbsp (30 ml) water

½ cup (67 g) frozen peas

Turn the Instant Pot on to sauté mode. Pat the meat dry with a paper towel to remove any excess moisture, then season with salt and pepper on all sides. Add the butter to the Instant Pot insert and sear the meat, working in batches if necessary, until golden brown on all sides. Add the carrots, potatoes, onion soup mix, tomatoes, balsamic vinegar and thyme and stir to combine. Seal the lid and turn the valve to the sealing position. Turn the Instant Pot on manual, high pressure for 40 minutes. Release the pressure manually by carefully moving the valve to venting. Turn the Instant Pot on to sauté mode again and add the cornstarch mixture along with the frozen peas. Stir for 3 minutes until thickened.

MEXICAN BEEF STEW

1 lb (454 g) beef stew meat

Kosher salt and black pepper

1 tbsp (14 g) unsalted butter

2 cups (256 g) carrots, diced

2 cups (300 g) Russet potatoes, peeled, diced in 1-inch (3-cm) chunks

1 (1-oz [28-g]) packet taco seasoning

1 (14.5-oz [411-g]) can diced tomatoes, drained

1 cup (240 ml) red salsa

1 cup (240 ml) lager beer or beef stock

1 tbsp (8 g) cornstarch mixed with 2 tbsp (30 ml) water

Turn the Instant Pot on to sauté mode. Pat the meat dry with a paper towel to remove any excess moisture, then season with salt and pepper on all sides. Add the butter to the Instant Pot insert and sear the meat, working in batches if necessary, until golden brown on all sides. Add the carrots, potatoes, taco seasoning, tomatoes, salsa and beer and stir to combine. Seal the lid and turn the valve to the sealing position. Turn the Instant Pot on manual, high pressure for 40 minutes. Release the pressure manually by carefully moving the valve to venting. Turn the Instant Pot on to sauté mode again and add the cornstarch mixture. Stir for 3 minutes until thickened.

RAMEN

YIELD: 4 SERVINGS

My son Logan asks for ramen once a week. This Instant Pot version is so much healthier than the packaged ramen and tastes a million times better. His favorite is the Chicken Ramen (page 74). This recipe gets some help from the delicious ramen broth you can find in most grocery stores now. It's quick to make and the perfect comfort food.

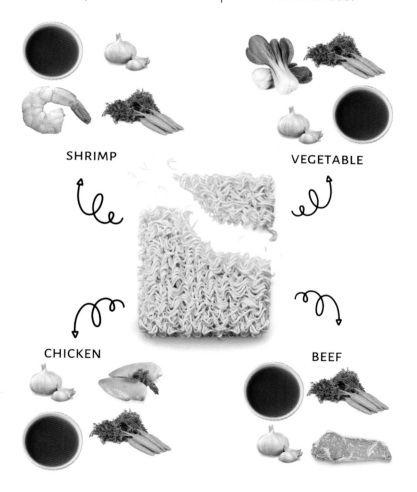

SHRIMP

VEGETABLE

CHICKEN

BEEF

CHICKEN RAMEN

1 lb (454 g) chicken breasts, cut in half lengthwise to create four thin cutlets

Kosher salt and pepper

1 tsp avocado or olive oil

3 tbsp (42 g) unsalted butter

2 cloves garlic, minced

5 dry shiitake mushrooms

2 (26-oz [737-g]) cartons ramen broth

½ cup (64 g) carrots, julienned

8 oz (226 g) dry ramen noodles

¼ cup (12 g) green onions, sliced

Turn the Instant Pot on to sauté mode. Season the chicken with salt and pepper on both sides. Add the oil and chicken to the pot and brown for 5 to 7 minutes per side, or until the chicken is cooked through. Remove the chicken and set aside. Add the butter, garlic and mushrooms and sauté for 5 minutes. Add the broth and seal with the lid. Turn the valve to the sealing position and cook on manual, high pressure for 5 minutes.

Meanwhile, slice the chicken into bite-sized pieces. Remove the lid and turn the pot back on to sauté mode. Remove the mushrooms and slice thinly. Add the mushrooms back to the pot along with the carrots and noodles and cook for 3 minutes. Top the ramen with the chicken and green onions.

*See image on page 72.

BEEF RAMEN

1 (32-oz [907-g]) New York strip steak

Kosher salt and pepper

1 tsp avocado or olive oil

3 tbsp (42 g) unsalted butter

2 cloves garlic, minced

5 dry shiitake mushrooms

2 (26-oz [737-g]) cartons ramen broth

½ cup (64 g) carrots, julienned

8 oz (226 g) dry ramen noodles

¼ cup (12 g) green onions, sliced

Turn the Instant Pot on to sauté mode. Pat the steak dry with a paper towel to remove any excess moisture, then season with salt and pepper on both sides. Add the oil and steak to the pot and brown for 5 to 7 minutes per side. Remove the steak and set aside to rest. Add the butter, garlic and mushrooms to the pot and sauté for 5 minutes. Add the ramen broth and seal with the lid. Turn the valve to the sealing position and cook on manual, high pressure for 5 minutes.

Meanwhile, slice the steak into bite-sized pieces. Remove the lid and turn the pot back on to sauté mode. Remove the mushrooms and slice thinly. Add the mushrooms back to the pot along with the carrots and noodles and cook for 3 minutes. Top the ramen with the steak and green onions.

SHRIMP RAMEN

1 lb (454 g) raw shrimp, peeled and deveined

Kosher salt and pepper

1 tsp avocado or olive oil

3 tbsp (42 g) unsalted butter

2 cloves garlic, minced

5 dry shiitake mushrooms

2 (26-oz [737-g]) cartons ramen broth

½ cup (64 g) carrots, julienned

8 oz (226 g) dry ramen noodles

¼ cup (12 g) green onions, sliced

Turn the Instant Pot on to sauté mode. Pat the shrimp dry with a paper towel, then season it with salt and pepper on both sides. Add the oil and shrimp to the pot and cook for 5 to 7 minutes. Remove the shrimp and set aside. Add the butter, garlic and mushrooms and sauté for 5 minutes. Add the ramen broth and seal with the lid. Turn the valve to the sealing position and cook on manual, high pressure for 5 minutes. Remove the lid and turn the pot back on to sauté mode. Remove the mushrooms and slice thinly. Add the mushrooms back to the pot along with the carrots and noodles and cook for 3 minutes. Top the ramen with the shrimp and green onions.

VEGETABLE RAMEN

3 tbsp (42 g) unsalted butter

2 cloves garlic, minced

5 dry shiitake mushrooms

2 (26-oz [737-g]) cartons ramen broth

½ cup (64 g) carrots, julienned

2 heads of bok choy, chopped into 1-inch (3-cm) pieces

8 oz (226 g) dry ramen noodles

¼ cup (12 g) green onions, sliced

Turn the Instant Pot on to sauté mode. Add the butter, garlic and mushrooms and sauté for 5 minutes. Add the broth and seal with the lid. Turn the valve to the sealing position and cook on manual, high pressure for 5 minutes. Remove the lid and turn the pot back on to sauté mode. Remove the mushrooms and slice thinly. Add the mushrooms back to the pot along with the carrots, bok choy and noodles and cook for 3 minutes. Top the ramen with the green onions.

POTATO SOUP

Creamy potato soup is a perfect blank canvas for yummy toppings.
My favorite topping, the Italian Sausage and Kale (page 78), brings me
straight back to a trattoria where I used to eat in Florence, Italy, while I was in
culinary school. You can make a big batch and freeze leftovers as well.

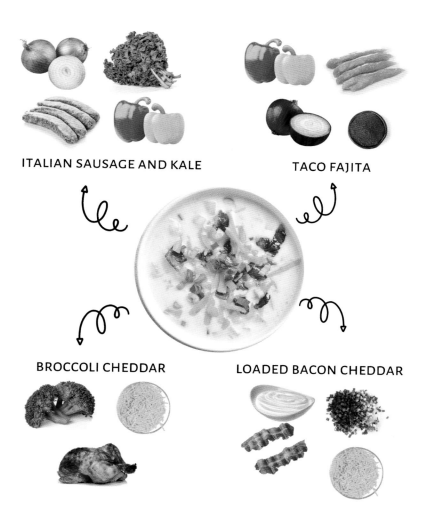

ITALIAN SAUSAGE AND KALE

TACO FAJITA

BROCCOLI CHEDDAR

LOADED BACON CHEDDAR

ITALIAN SAUSAGE AND KALE POTATO SOUP

3 tbsp (42 g) unsalted butter
1 cup (160 g) onions, diced
2 tsp (5 g) all-purpose flour
10 cups (1.5 kg) Russet potatoes, peeled and quartered
2 tbsp plus 1 tsp (42 g) kosher salt, divided
4 cups (960 ml) chicken stock
1 cup (240 ml) heavy cream
¼ tsp black pepper
1 tsp olive oil
1 lb (454 g) Italian sausage
½ cup (57 g) white onion, sliced thinly
½ cup red bell pepper, sliced thinly
1 cup (67 g) kale, roughly chopped

Turn the Instant Pot on to sauté mode. Add the butter and onions and sauté for 3 minutes. Add the flour and stir to combine. Add the potatoes, 2 tablespoons (36 g) of the salt and the stock. Seal with the lid and cook on manual, high pressure for 20 minutes. Manually release the pressure by carefully moving the valve to the venting position. Add the cream, remaining teaspoon of salt and the pepper and blend with an immersion blender until smooth. If you do not have an immersion blender you can use a blender. Just be sure to blend in small batches and let the steam escape from the lid.

Remove the soup from the Instant Pot and clean the insert. For the topping, turn the Instant Pot on to sauté mode. Add the oil and sausage and cook until browned, breaking it up into pieces while cooking. Add the onion and bell pepper and cook for an additional 3 minutes. Add the kale and cook until slightly wilted, about 1 to 2 minutes. Serve on top of the potato soup.

See image on page 76.

TACO FAJITA POTATO SOUP

3 tbsp (42 g) unsalted butter
1 cup (160 g) onions, diced
2 tsp (5 g) all-purpose flour
10 cups (1.5 kg) Russet potatoes, peeled and quartered
2 tbsp plus 1 tsp (42 g) kosher salt, divided
4 cups (960 ml) chicken stock
1 cup (240 ml) heavy cream
¼ tsp black pepper
1 tbsp (15 ml) avocado or olive oil
1 lb (454 g) chicken tenders
Taco seasoning, to taste
½ cup (57 g) red onion, sliced thinly
½ cup (60 g) red bell pepper, sliced thinly
½ cup (60 g) yellow bell pepper, sliced thinly

Turn the Instant Pot on to sauté mode. Add the butter and onions and sauté for 3 minutes. Add the flour and stir to combine. Add the potatoes, 2 tablespoons (36 g) of the salt and the stock. Seal with the lid and cook on manual, high pressure for 20 minutes. Manually release the pressure by carefully moving the valve to the venting position. Add the cream, remaining teaspoon of salt and the pepper and blend with an immersion blender until smooth. If you do not have an immersion blender you can use a blender. Just be sure to blend in small batches and let the steam escape from the lid.

Remove the soup from the Instant Pot and clean the insert. For the topping, turn the Instant Pot on to sauté mode. Add the oil and chicken tenders and season with the taco seasoning. Cook until browned and cooked through, about 10 minutes. Remove the chicken from the pot and dice. Add the onion and bell peppers and cook for an additional 5 to 7 minutes. Add the chicken to the onion and bell pepper mix and stir to combine. Serve on top of the potato soup.

BROCCOLI-CHEDDAR POTATO SOUP

5 tbsp (70 g) unsalted butter, divided
1 cup (160 g) onions, diced
2 tsp (5 g) all-purpose flour
10 cups (1.5 kg) Russet potatoes, peeled and quartered
2 tbsp plus 1 tsp (42 g) kosher salt, divided, plus more to taste
4 cups (960 ml) chicken stock
1 cup (240 ml) heavy cream
¼ tsp black pepper, plus more to taste
1 cup (125 g) rotisserie chicken
1 cup (91 g) broccoli, roughly chopped
1 cup (113 g) shredded cheddar cheese

Turn the Instant Pot on to sauté mode. Add 3 tablespoons (42 g) of the butter and the onions and sauté for 3 minutes. Add the flour and stir to combine. Add the potatoes, 2 tablespoons (36 g) of the salt and the stock. Seal with the lid and cook on manual, high pressure for 20 minutes. Manually release the pressure by carefully moving the valve to the venting position. Add the cream, remaining teaspoon of salt and the pepper and blend with an immersion blender until smooth. If you do not have an immersion blender you can use a blender. Just be sure to blend in small batches and let the steam escape from the lid.

Remove the soup from the Instant Pot and clean the insert. For the topping, turn the Instant Pot on to sauté mode. Add the remaining 2 tablespoons (28 g) of butter, the chicken and broccoli, then season with salt and pepper to taste. Cover with the lid and cook for 2 minutes to steam the broccoli. Serve the chicken and broccoli mixture on top of the potato soup and top with the cheddar cheese.

LOADED BACON CHEDDAR POTATO SOUP

3 tbsp (42 g) unsalted butter
1 cup (160 g) onions, diced
2 tsp (5 g) all-purpose flour
10 cups (1.5 kg) Russet potatoes, peeled and quartered
2 tbsp plus 1 tsp (42 g) kosher salt, divided
4 cups (960 ml) chicken stock
1 cup (240 ml) heavy cream
¼ tsp black pepper
1 lb (454 g) applewood smoked bacon, cooked until crispy and roughly chopped
1 cup (113 g) shredded cheddar cheese
Sour cream, to taste
¼ cup (12 g) chives, chopped

Turn the Instant Pot on to sauté mode. Add the butter and onions and sauté for 3 minutes. Add the flour and stir to combine. Add the potatoes, 2 tablespoons (36 g) of the salt and the stock. Seal with the lid and cook on manual, high pressure for 20 minutes. Manually release the pressure by carefully moving the valve to the venting position. Add the cream, the remaining teaspoon of salt and the pepper and blend with an immersion blender until smooth. If you do not have an immersion blender you can use a blender. Just be sure to blend in small batches and let the steam escape from the lid.

Top the soup with the bacon, cheese, sour cream and chives.

TOMATO SOUP

YIELD: 6 SERVINGS

Tomato soup is one of those comforting meals that everybody loves. Make this delicious base recipe and then top your soup with the fun topping ideas listed below. It is important to follow the directions exactly to prevent getting a burn notice on your Instant Pot. Thicker ingredients like tomatoes can burn easily because they release moisture more slowly than other ingredients.

BACON, AVOCADO AND CROUTONS

CHICKEN PARMESAN TOPPING

GRILLED CHEESE CROUTONS

MOZZARELLA TOPPING

TOMATO SOUP WITH MOZZARELLA TOPPING

FOR THE TOMATO SOUP BASE

1 tsp olive oil

1 cup (160 g) white onion, diced

1 cup (101 g) celery, diced

2 cups (256 g) carrots, peeled and diced

3 cloves garlic, peeled and crushed

1 cup (240 ml) chicken stock

2 (12-oz [340-g]) cans peeled plum tomatoes

1 tbsp (15 g) granulated sugar

¾ cup (180 ml) heavy cream

1–2 tsp (6–12 g) kosher salt, or to taste

4 leaves fresh basil

FOR THE MOZZARELLA TOPPING

1 cup (226 g) diced fresh mozzarella

3 fresh basil leaves, sliced into chiffonade (see Note on page 44)

1 tbsp (15 ml) extra-virgin olive oil

Kosher salt and pepper, to taste

Balsamic glaze, for garnish

Turn the Instant Pot on to sauté mode. Add the oil, onion, celery, carrots and garlic and sauté for 5 to 7 minutes, or until the onion is soft. Add the stock and tomatoes, but do not stir. Seal the lid and turn the valve to the sealing position. Turn the Instant Pot on manual, high pressure for 10 minutes. Release the pressure manually by carefully moving the valve to venting. Add the sugar, cream, salt and basil and carefully blend with an immersion blender. Blend until smooth.

Combine the mozzarella with the basil and oil. Season with salt and pepper and toss to combine. Place the mozzarella mixture on top of the soup and drizzle with the balsamic glaze.

TOMATO SOUP WITH GRILLED CHEESE CROUTONS

FOR THE TOMATO SOUP BASE

1 tsp olive oil

1 cup (160 g) white onion, diced

1 cup (101 g) celery, diced

2 cups (256 g) carrots, peeled and diced

3 cloves garlic, peeled and crushed

1 cup (240 ml) chicken stock

2 (12-oz [340-g]) cans peeled plum tomatoes

1 tbsp (15 g) granulated sugar

¾ cup (180 ml) heavy cream

1–2 tsp (6–12 g) kosher salt, or to taste

4 leaves fresh basil

FOR THE GRILLED CHEESE CROUTONS

4 slices sourdough bread

1 cup (113 g) shredded cheddar cheese

½ cup (57 g) Monterey Jack cheese, shredded

2 tbsp (28 g) unsalted butter, softened

1 tbsp (6 g) Parmesan cheese, finely grated

Make the tomato soup base by following the instructions in the Mozzarella Topping variation.

Preheat a griddle or cast-iron skillet over medium heat. Place the bread on a clean work surface. Divide the cheddar and Monterey Jack cheeses between two slices of bread. Top with the remaining bread slices. In a small bowl, combine the butter and Parmesan, then spread the mixture on the exposed side of each of the slices of bread. Place the sandwiches on the griddle and cook for 3 minutes per side or until the bread is toasted and the cheese is melted. Let the sandwiches cool slightly and cut them into 1-inch (3-cm) squares. Place the grilled cheese croutons on top of the soup to serve.

TOMATO SOUP WITH BACON, AVOCADO AND CROUTONS

FOR THE TOMATO SOUP BASE

1 tsp olive oil

1 cup (160 g) white onion, diced

1 cup (101 g) celery, diced

2 cups (256 g) carrots, peeled and diced

3 cloves garlic, peeled and crushed

1 cup (240 ml) chicken stock

2 (12-oz [340-g]) cans peeled plum tomatoes

1 tbsp (15 g) granulated sugar

¾ cup (180 ml) heavy cream

1–2 tsp (6–12 g) kosher salt, or to taste

4 leaves fresh basil

FOR THE BACON, AVOCADO AND CROUTON TOPPING

4 slices bacon, cooked until crispy and roughly chopped

1 avocado, pitted and diced

1 cup (30 g) premade croutons

Zest of 1 lemon (see Notes)

Make the tomato soup base by following the instructions in the Mozzarella Topping variation (page 82).

Top your soup bowls with the desired amount of chopped bacon, avocado and croutons. Zest the lemon straight over the topping.

NOTES

Lemon zest adds a bright flavor and helps cut the fattiness of the avocado.

To zest a lemon, rotate the lemon on a rasp grater, making sure to only grate the bright yellow zest. You do not want the pith, or white part, of the lemon, as it can be bitter.

TOMATO SOUP WITH CHICKEN PARMESAN TOPPING

FOR THE TOMATO SOUP BASE

1 tsp olive oil

1 cup (160 g) white onion, diced

1 cup (101 g) celery, diced

2 cups (256 g) carrots, peeled and diced

3 cloves garlic, peeled and crushed

1 cup (240 ml) chicken stock

2 (12-oz [340-g]) cans peeled plum tomatoes

1 tbsp (15 g) granulated sugar

¾ cup (180 ml) heavy cream

1–2 tsp (6–12 g) kosher salt, or to taste

4 leaves fresh basil

FOR THE CHICKEN PARMESAN TOPPING

1 cup (56 g) panko bread crumbs

1 lb (454 g) boneless, skinless chicken breasts, sliced in half lengthwise, to make 4 thin cutlets

Kosher salt and pepper

2 tbsp (30 ml) avocado or olive oil

½ cup (50 g) Parmesan cheese, shredded

Make the tomato soup base by following the instructions in the Mozzarella Topping variation (page 82).

To make the topping, preheat the oven to 400°F (204°C). Pour the bread crumbs into a shallow baking dish. Using the flat side of a meat tenderizer or your fist, pound the chicken in between two pieces of parchment paper. Dredge the chicken in the bread crumbs, pressing down firmly and coating both sides. Season with salt and pepper.

Meanwhile, preheat a large, nonstick skillet over medium heat. Add the oil and place the chicken onto the preheated pan. Sear for 7 minutes per side. Remove the chicken from the pan and roughly chop it into 1-inch (3-cm) pieces. Top the soup with the chicken and Parmesan.

*See image on page 80.

CREAM OF...

These creamy soups are the perfect healthy substitutes to canned "cream of" soups. I love making a big batch of Cream of Chicken Soup (page 86) and serving it over Coconut Rice (page 195) with a variety of toppings like pineapple, celery, cheddar cheese and crunchy chow mein noodles, which makes a quick family-friendly dinner.

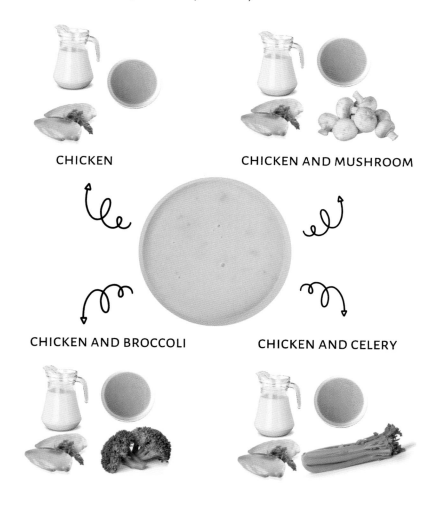

CHICKEN

CHICKEN AND MUSHROOM

CHICKEN AND BROCCOLI

CHICKEN AND CELERY

CREAM OF CHICKEN SOUP

3 tbsp (42 g) unsalted butter

1½ lbs (680 g) boneless, skinless chicken breast

3 tbsp (24 g) all-purpose flour

4 cups (960 ml) chicken stock

1 cup (240 ml) heavy cream

2 tbsp (16 g) cornstarch mixed with 2 tbsp (30 ml) cold water

Kosher salt and pepper, to taste

Turn the Instant Pot on to sauté mode. Melt the butter and sauté the chicken for 3 minutes per side. Add the flour and stir to combine. Add the stock, seal the lid and turn the valve to the sealing position. Turn the Instant Pot on manual, high pressure for 10 minutes. Release the pressure manually by carefully moving the valve to venting.

Remove the chicken and cut it into small pieces. It is okay if it's not fully cooked, as it will continue to cook on sauté mode. Turn the pot on to sauté mode and add the cream, cornstarch mixture and diced chicken. Cook for 5 minutes to thicken, then season with salt and pepper to taste. Make sure the chicken is cooked through.

See image on page 84.

CREAM OF CHICKEN AND MUSHROOM SOUP

5 tbsp (70 g) unsalted butter, divided

3 cups (210 g) button mushrooms, sliced thinly

1½ lbs (680 g) boneless, skinless chicken breast

3 tbsp (24 g) all-purpose flour

4 cups (960 ml) chicken stock

1 cup (240 ml) heavy cream

2 tbsp (16 g) cornstarch mixed with 2 tbsp (30 ml) cold water

Kosher salt and pepper, to taste

Turn the Instant Pot on to sauté mode. Melt 2 tablespoons (28 g) of butter and sauté the mushrooms for 5 minutes. Remove the mushrooms and set aside. Add the remaining 3 tablespoons (42 g) of butter and the chicken to the pot. Sauté the chicken for 3 minutes per side. Add the flour and stir to combine. Add the stock, seal the lid and turn the valve to the sealing position. Turn the Instant Pot on manual, high pressure for 10 minutes. Release the pressure manually by carefully moving the valve to venting.

Remove the chicken and cut into small pieces. It is okay if it's not fully cooked, as it will continue to cook on sauté mode. Turn the pot on to sauté mode and add the cream, cornstarch mixture, the diced chicken and reserved mushrooms. Cook for 5 minutes to thicken, then season with salt and pepper to taste. Make sure the chicken is cooked through.

CREAM OF CHICKEN AND BROCCOLI SOUP

3 tbsp (42 g) unsalted butter

1½ lbs (680 g) boneless, skinless chicken breast

3 tbsp (24 g) all-purpose flour

4 cups (960 ml) chicken stock

1 cup (240 ml) heavy cream

2 tbsp (16 g) cornstarch mixed with 2 tbsp (30 ml) cold water

4 cups (364 g) broccoli, finely chopped

Kosher salt and pepper, to taste

Turn the Instant Pot on to sauté mode. Melt the butter and sauté the chicken for 3 minutes per side. Add the flour and stir to combine. Add the stock, seal the lid and turn the valve to the sealing position. Turn the Instant Pot on manual, high pressure for 10 minutes. Release the pressure manually by carefully moving the valve to venting.

Remove the chicken and cut it into small pieces. It is okay if it's not fully cooked, as it will continue to cook on sauté mode. Turn the pot on to sauté mode and add the cream, cornstarch mixture, chicken and broccoli. Cook for 5 minutes to thicken, then season with salt and pepper to taste. Make sure the chicken is cooked through.

CREAM OF CHICKEN AND CELERY SOUP

5 tbsp (70 g) unsalted butter, divided

4 cups (404 g) celery, diced small

1½ lbs (680 g) boneless, skinless chicken breast

3 tbsp (24 g) all-purpose flour

4 cups (960 ml) chicken stock

1 cup (240 ml) heavy cream

2 tbsp (16 g) cornstarch mixed with 2 tbsp (30 ml) cold water

Kosher salt and pepper, to taste

Turn the Instant Pot on to sauté mode. Melt 2 tablespoons (28 g) of butter and sauté the celery for 3 minutes. Add the chicken and cook for 3 minutes per side. Add the remaining 3 tablespoons (42 g) of butter and the flour and stir to combine. Add the stock, seal the lid and turn the valve to the sealing position. Turn the Instant Pot on manual, high pressure for 10 minutes. Release the pressure manually by carefully moving the valve to venting.

Remove the chicken and cut it into small pieces. It is okay if it's not fully cooked, as it will continue to cook on sauté mode. Turn the pot on to sauté mode and add the cream, cornstarch mixture and chicken. Cook for 5 minutes to thicken, then season with salt and pepper to taste. Make sure the chicken is cooked through.

CHILI

YIELD: 6-8 SERVINGS

Try the pot-in-pot method with these recipes. Cook your chili on the bottom insert, add a high trivet and cook some cornbread on top of the trivet. You can cook your main dish and your side all in one.

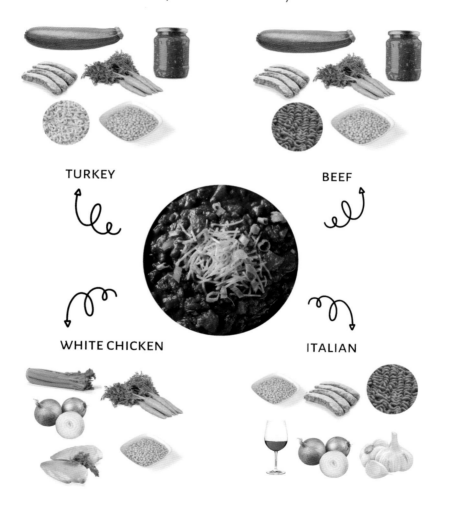

TURKEY

BEEF

WHITE CHICKEN

ITALIAN

TURKEY CHILI

1 lb (454 g) Italian sweet chicken sausage

1 lb (454 g) ground turkey

½ cup (80 g) white onion, diced

2 cloves garlic, minced

1 tsp onion powder

1 tbsp (7 g) chili powder

½ tsp dried oregano

½ tsp cumin

1 tsp smoked paprika

½ cup (64 g) carrots, shredded

½ cup (75 g) zucchini, shredded

1 (14.5-oz [411-g]) can diced tomatoes with juice

1 (15-oz [425-g]) can tomato sauce

1 (15.5-oz [439-g]) can cannellini beans, rinsed and drained

½ tbsp (7 ml) Dijon mustard

½ tbsp (7 ml) Worcestershire sauce

1 cup (240 ml) chicken stock

2 tsp (12 g) kosher salt

Corn chips, for serving (optional)

Shredded cheddar cheese, for serving (optional)

Sour cream, for serving (optional)

Diced avocado, for serving (optional)

Turn the Instant Pot on to sauté mode. Remove the sausage from the casing and brown it in the Instant Pot along with the turkey. Break the meat up into small pieces while browning. When the sausage is almost cooked, about 10 minutes, add the onion, garlic, onion powder, chili powder, oregano, cumin, paprika, carrots, zucchini, tomatoes, tomato sauce, beans, mustard, Worcestershire, stock and salt. Seal the lid and turn the valve to the sealing position. Turn the Instant Pot on manual, high pressure for 10 minutes. Release the pressure manually by carefully moving the valve to venting. Ladle the chili into your serving bowls and top with the optional toppings.

BEEF CHILI

1 lb (454 g) Italian sausage

1 lb (454 g) ground beef

½ cup (80 g) white onion, diced

2 cloves garlic, minced

1 tsp onion powder

1 tbsp (7 g) chili powder

½ tsp dried oregano

½ tsp cumin

1 tsp smoked paprika

½ cup (64 g) carrots, shredded

½ cup (75 g) zucchini, shredded

1 (14.5-oz [411-g]) can diced tomatoes with juice

1 (15-oz [425-g]) can tomato sauce

1 (15.5-oz [439-g]) can cannellini beans, rinsed and drained

½ tbsp (7 ml) Dijon mustard

½ tbsp (7 ml) Worcestershire sauce

1 cup (240 ml) chicken stock

2 tsp (12 g) kosher salt

Corn chips, for serving (optional)

Shredded cheddar cheese, for serving (optional)

Sour cream, for serving (optional)

Diced avocado, for serving (optional)

Turn the Instant Pot on to sauté mode. Remove the sausage from the casing and brown it in the Instant Pot along with the beef. Break the meat up into small pieces while browning. When the sausage is almost cooked, about 10 minutes, add the onion, garlic, dried spices, carrots, zucchini, tomatoes, tomato sauce, beans, mustard, Worcestershire, stock and salt. Seal the lid and turn the valve to the sealing position. Turn the Instant Pot on manual, high pressure for 10 minutes. Release the pressure manually by carefully moving the valve to venting. Ladle the chili into your serving bowls and top with the optional toppings.

WHITE CHICKEN CHILI

2 tbsp (28 g) unsalted butter

2 cups (320 g) white onion, diced

2 cups (256 g) carrots, diced

2 cups (202 g) celery, diced

4 cloves garlic, minced

2 lbs (907 g) boneless, skinless chicken breast, diced into ½-inch (1.3-cm) cubes

2 tbsp (16 g) all-purpose flour

1 tsp oregano

1 tsp onion powder

1 tsp garlic salt

¼ tsp cumin

4 oz (113 g) diced green chilies

1 (25-oz [708-g]) can Mexican-style hominy, rinsed and drained

1 (15.5-oz [439-g]) can cannellini beans, drained and rinsed

2 (32-oz [907-g]) containers chicken stock

3 tbsp (24 g) cornstarch mixed with 3 tbsp (45 ml) cold water

½ cup (120 ml) heavy cream

Kosher salt and pepper, to taste

Corn chips, for serving (optional)

Chopped cilantro, for serving (optional)

Turn the Instant Pot on to sauté mode. Melt the butter in the insert. Add the onion, carrots, celery and garlic and sauté for 3 minutes. Add the chicken and sauté for an additional 3 minutes. Sprinkle with the flour, oregano, onion powder, garlic salt and cumin and stir to combine. Add the green chilies, hominy, beans and stock.

Seal the lid and turn the valve to the sealing position. Turn the Instant Pot on manual, high pressure for 10 minutes. Release the pressure manually by carefully moving the valve to venting. Turn the Instant Pot back on to sauté mode and add the cornstarch mixture, cream and salt and pepper to taste. Cook for an additional 3 minutes to thicken. Ladle into bowls and add the optional toppings.

See image on page 88.

ITALIAN CHILI

1 tsp avocado or olive oil

1 cup (160 g) white onion, diced small

2 cloves garlic, minced

1 lb (454 g) sweet Italian sausage

1 lb (454 g) ground beef

1 (15.5-oz [439-g]) can white beans, rinsed and drained

1 cup (240 ml) red cooking wine

1 (28-oz [794-g]) can Italian-style peeled tomatoes

1 tsp kosher salt

¼ cup (55 g) tomato paste

Splash of heavy whipping cream (optional)

Turn the Instant Pot on to sauté mode. Place the oil, onion and garlic in the pot and sauté for 1 to 2 minutes, or until the onion is translucent. Remove the sausage from the casing and add it to the pot, along with the ground beef. Cook until the meat is almost cooked through, about 10 minutes, breaking the meat into small pieces while cooking. Add the beans, wine, tomatoes, salt and tomato paste. Cook on manual, high pressure for 20 minutes. Release the pressure manually by carefully moving the valve to venting. Stir in the cream if desired.

CASSEROLES

Creamy, delicious casseroles can feed a crowd in minutes. It's a one-pot meal that goes a long way. I love casseroles in the Instant Pot because they never dry out! So many times casseroles can dry out in the oven because of the dry heat, but using the Instant Pot always makes for a moist and delicious casserole.

POT PIE

YIELD: 6 SERVINGS

I love pot pie because it's a quick comfort food in which you can change up the flavors easily. A family favorite is the Cauliflower Pot Pie (page 96). It's a meatless version that my kids can't even tell is full of vegetables.

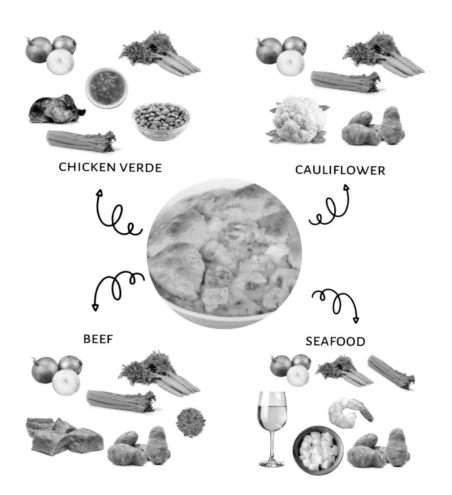

CHICKEN VERDE

CAULIFLOWER

BEEF

SEAFOOD

CHICKEN VERDE POT PIE

5 tbsp (70 g) unsalted butter, divided
1 cup (128 g) carrots, peeled and diced
1 cup (160 g) white onion, diced
1 cup (101 g) celery, diced
2½ tbsp (20 g) all-purpose flour
4 cups (500 g) rotisserie chicken, shredded
3 cups (720 ml) chicken stock
1 (10-oz [283-g]) can green enchilada sauce or salsa verde
1 (16.3-oz [462-g]) can premade biscuits
1 tsp taco seasoning
2 tbsp (16 g) cornstarch mixed with 2 tbsp (30 ml) water
1 (15.5-oz [439-g]) can pinto beans, rinsed and drained
Chopped cilantro, for topping (optional)
Crumbled cotija cheese, for topping (optional)

Turn the Instant Pot on to sauté mode. Add 2 tablespoons (28 g) of the butter to melt. When the butter is melted, add the carrots, onion and celery and sauté for 5 minutes. Add the flour and stir to combine. Cook for 2 minutes. Add the chicken, stock and enchilada sauce and stir to combine.

Place a high trivet in the pot. Place the canned biscuits in a cake pan that fits inside the Instant Pot insert. Melt the remaining 3 tablespoons (42 g) of butter, and brush it over the top of the biscuits, then season with taco seasoning. Cover with a paper towel and then with foil and place the cake pan on top of the trivet. Seal the lid and turn the valve to the sealing position. Turn the Instant Pot on manual, high pressure for 20 minutes. Release the pressure manually by carefully moving the valve to venting.

Remove the cake pan and trivet. Add the cornstarch mixture and beans and turn the Instant Pot on to sauté mode for 3 minutes to thicken. Serve the pot pie with the biscuits and topped with cilantro and cotija cheese, if using.

*See image on page 94.

CAULIFLOWER POT PIE

6 tbsp (84 g) unsalted butter, divided
2 cups (256 g) carrots, peeled and diced
1 cup (160 g) white onion, diced
2 cups (202 g) celery, diced
3 tbsp (24 g) all-purpose flour
4 cups (400 g) cauliflower, roughly chopped
2 cups (300 g) Russet potatoes, peeled and diced into ½-inch (1.3-cm) cubes
2 cups (480 ml) chicken stock
1 (16.3-oz [462-g]) can premade biscuits
2 tsp (12 g) kosher salt
¼ tsp black pepper
2 tbsp (16 g) cornstarch mixed with 2 tbsp (30 ml) water

Turn the Instant Pot on to sauté mode. Add 3 tablespoons (42 g) of butter and when melted add the carrots, onion and celery and sauté for 5 minutes. Add the flour and stir to combine. Cook for 2 minutes. Add the cauliflower, potatoes and stock and stir to combine.

Place a high trivet in the pot. Place the canned biscuits in a cake pan that fits inside the Instant Pot insert. Melt the remaining 3 tablespoons (42 g) of butter, and brush it over the top of the biscuits. Cover with a paper towel and then with foil and place the pan on top of the trivet. Seal the lid and turn the valve to the sealing position. Turn the Instant Pot on manual, high pressure for 10 minutes. Release the pressure manually by carefully moving the valve to venting.

Remove the cake pan and trivet. Add the salt, pepper and cornstarch mixture and turn the Instant Pot on to sauté mode for 3 minutes to thicken. Serve the pot pie with the biscuits.

BEEF POT PIE

5 tbsp (70 g) unsalted butter, divided
1½ lbs (680 g) beef stew meat
3 tbsp (24 g) all-purpose flour
Kosher salt and black pepper, to taste
2 cups (256 g) carrots, peeled and diced
1 cup (160 g) white onion, diced
2 cups (202 g) celery, diced
2 cups (300 g) Russet potatoes, peeled and diced into ½-inch (1.3-cm) cubes
2 cups (480 ml) beef stock
1 tsp kosher salt
1 tsp Italian seasoning
1 (16.3-oz [462-g]) can premade biscuits
2 tbsp (16 g) cornstarch mixed with 2 tbsp (30 ml) water

Turn the Instant Pot on to sauté mode. Add 2 tablespoons (28 g) of butter to melt. Pat the stew meat dry with a paper towel. Coat the meat in the flour and season with salt and pepper to taste. When the butter is melted, add the carrots, onion and celery and sauté for 5 minutes. Add the potatoes, stock, salt and Italian seasoning and stir to combine.

Place a high trivet in the pot. Place the canned biscuits in a cake pan that fits inside the Instant Pot insert. Melt the remaining 3 tablespoons (42 g) of butter and brush it over the tops of the biscuits. Cover with a paper towel and then with foil and place the pan on top of the trivet. Seal the lid and turn the valve to the sealing position. Turn the Instant Pot on manual, high pressure for 45 minutes. Release the pressure manually by carefully moving the valve to venting.

Remove the cake pan and trivet. Add the cornstarch mixture and turn the Instant Pot on to sauté mode for 3 minutes to thicken. Serve the pot pie with the biscuits.

SEAFOOD POT PIE

5 tbsp (70 g) unsalted butter, divided
1 cup (128 g) carrots, peeled and diced
1 cup (160 g) white onion, diced
1 cup (101 g) celery, diced
2½ tbsp (20 g) all-purpose flour
2 cups (300 g) Russet potatoes, peeled and diced into ½-inch (1.3-cm) cubes
1 cup (240 ml) white wine
2 cups (480 ml) chicken stock
1 tsp kosher salt
⅛ tsp black pepper
1 (16.3-oz [462-g]) can premade biscuits
½ lb (226 g) raw frozen shrimp, peeled and deveined
½ lb (226 g) frozen scallops
2 tbsp (16 g) cornstarch mixed with 2 tbsp (30 ml) water

Turn the Instant Pot on to sauté mode. Add 2 tablespoons (28 g) of the butter and when melted add the carrots, onion and celery and sauté for 5 minutes. Add the flour and stir to combine. Cook for 2 minutes. Add the potatoes, wine, stock, salt and pepper and stir to combine.

Place a high trivet in the pot. Place the canned biscuits in a cake pan that fits inside the Instant Pot insert. Melt the remaining 3 tablespoons (42 g) of butter and brush it over the tops of the biscuits. Cover with a paper towel and then with foil and place the pan on top of the trivet. Seal the lid and turn the valve to the sealing position. Turn the Instant Pot on manual, high pressure for 10 minutes. Release the pressure manually by carefully moving the valve to venting.

Remove the cake pan and trivet. Add the shrimp, scallops and cornstarch mixture and turn the Instant Pot on to sauté mode for 5 minutes to cook the seafood. Serve the pot pie with the biscuits.

CHICKEN
AND RICE

YIELD: 6-8 SERVINGS

Creamy chicken and rice is a great casserole to make ahead of time.
I love to make extra and freeze it to take to people in need.
It's also a great meal to feed a crowd.

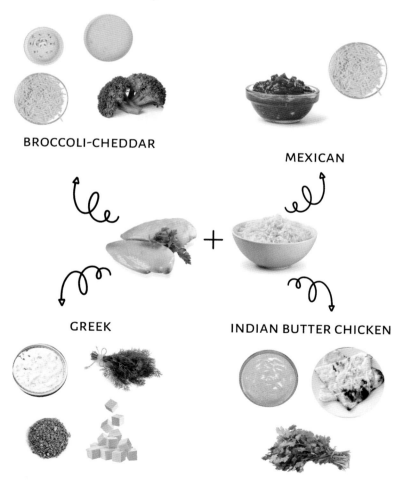

BROCCOLI-CHEDDAR

MEXICAN

GREEK

INDIAN BUTTER CHICKEN

BROCCOLI-CHEDDAR CHICKEN AND RICE CASSEROLE

1 tbsp (14 g) unsalted butter

1 lb (454 g) boneless, skinless chicken breast, cubed into small pieces

Kosher salt and black pepper

2 cups (200 g) white rice, rinsed with cold water

2 cups (480 ml) water

2 cups (174 g) frozen broccoli, thawed and roughly chopped

2 cups (226 g) shredded cheddar cheese, plus more to top

1 (12-oz [340-g]) can cream of chicken condensed soup

1 (12-oz [340-g]) can cream of mushroom condensed soup

Turn the Instant Pot on to sauté mode. Add the butter. Season the chicken with salt and pepper and sauté until browned and cooked through, about 7 minutes. Remove the chicken from the pot and set aside. Place the rinsed rice and water into the Instant Pot insert. Seal the lid and turn the valve to the sealing position. Cook on manual, high pressure for 10 minutes. Release the pressure naturally for 10 minutes.

Remove the lid and stir in the chicken, broccoli, cheddar cheese and soups and top with extra cheese. Place the lid back on the Instant Pot and let sit for 5 minutes or until the cheese is melted.

MEXICAN CHICKEN AND RICE CASSEROLE

1 tbsp (14 g) unsalted butter

1 lb (454 g) boneless, skinless chicken breast, cubed into small pieces

Kosher salt and black pepper

2 cups (200 g) white rice, rinsed with cold water

2 cups (480 ml) water

1 (12-oz [340-g]) jar of red salsa

2 cups (226 g) shredded cheddar cheese

Turn the Instant Pot on to sauté mode. Add the butter. Season the chicken with salt and pepper and sauté until browned and cooked through, about 7 minutes. Remove the chicken from the pot and set aside. Place the rinsed rice, water and salsa into the Instant Pot insert. Seal the lid and turn the valve to the sealing position. Cook on manual, high pressure for 10 minutes. Release the pressure naturally for 10 minutes.

Remove the lid, fluff the rice and stir in the chicken and cheddar cheese.

GREEK CHICKEN AND RICE CASSEROLE

1 tbsp (14 g) unsalted butter

1 lb (454 g) boneless, skinless chicken breast, cubed into small pieces

Kosher salt and black pepper

2 cups (200 g) white rice, rinsed with cold water

2 cups (480 ml) water

1 cube (11 g) chicken bouillon

1 tsp dried oregano

1 tbsp (3 g) fresh dill

¼ cup (38 g) fresh feta cheese, crumbled

FOR THE TZATZIKI SAUCE

2 cups (480 ml) plain Greek yogurt

1 cup (104 g) English cucumber, finely shredded and drained of excess liquid

1 tbsp (3 g) fresh dill, roughly chopped

1 tsp kosher salt

¼ tsp black pepper

1 tsp garlic, minced

Zest of 2 lemons

Turn the Instant Pot on to sauté mode. Add the butter. Season the chicken with salt and pepper and sauté until browned and cooked through, about 7 minutes. Remove the chicken from the pot and set aside. Place the rinsed rice, water, bouillon and oregano into the Instant Pot insert. Seal the lid and turn the valve to the sealing position. Cook on manual, high pressure for 5 minutes. Release the pressure naturally for 10 minutes. Remove the lid and fluff the rice. Top with the chicken, dill and feta cheese.

To make the tzatziki, in a small bowl combine the yogurt, cucumber, dill, salt, pepper, garlic and lemon zest and serve with chicken and rice.

See image on page 98.

INDIAN BUTTER CHICKEN AND RICE CASSEROLE

2 tbsp (28 g) unsalted butter

1 lb (454 g) boneless, skinless chicken breast, cubed into small pieces

Kosher salt and black pepper

2 cups (200 g) white rice, rinsed with cold water

2 cups (480 ml) water

1 (15-oz [425-g]) jar Indian butter chicken sauce

2 tsp (1 g) cilantro, roughly chopped

Premade naan bread, for serving

Turn the Instant Pot on to sauté mode. Add the butter. Season the chicken with salt and pepper and sauté until browned and cooked through, about 7 minutes. Remove the chicken from the pot and set aside. Place the rinsed rice, water and butter sauce into the Instant Pot insert. Seal the lid and turn the valve to the sealing position. Cook on manual, high pressure for 10 minutes. Release the pressure naturally for 10 minutes.

Remove the lid and fluff the rice. Stir in the chicken. Season with salt to taste and top with the cilantro. Serve with naan bread.

PIZZA PASTA CASSEROLE

YIELD: 4–6 SERVINGS

Pizza meets pasta and in an amazing way! This is one of my favorite ways to curb my pizza craving quickly. The Works Pizza Pasta Casserole (page 104) has become a Friday night tradition as of late. It's full of meat and vegetables and tastes just like a works pizza.

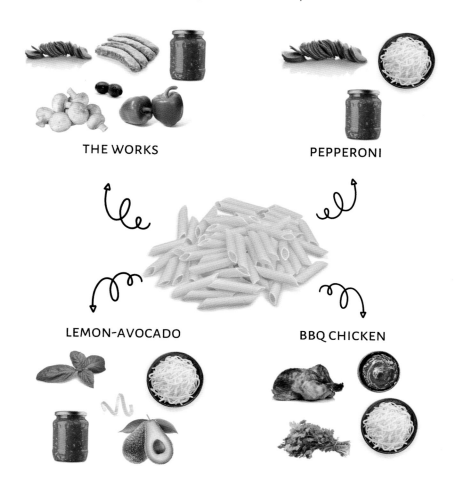

THE WORKS

PEPPERONI

LEMON-AVOCADO

BBQ CHICKEN

THE WORKS PIZZA PASTA CASSEROLE

1 lb (454 g) Italian sausage
½ cup (37 g) green bell peppers, diced
1 cup (70 g) mushrooms, sliced
¼ cup (30 g) pepperoni slices, quartered
3 cups (720 ml) water
1 lb (454 g) penne pasta
24 oz (679 g) tomato sauce
8 oz (226 g) shredded Italian five cheese blend
1 tbsp (8 g) black olives, sliced

Turn the Instant Pot on to sauté mode. Brown the sausage, breaking it up into small pieces while cooking. Once the sausage is browned, about 10 minutes, add the peppers, mushrooms, pepperoni and water and pull up any bits from the bottom of the pot with a wooden spoon. Add the penne and top with the tomato sauce. Seal the lid and turn the valve to the sealing position. Cook on manual, high pressure for 2 minutes. Release the pressure manually by carefully moving the valve to venting. Add the cheese blend and black olives and stir to combine.

*See image on page 102.

PEPPERONI PIZZA PASTA CASSEROLE

3 cups (720 ml) water
1 lb (454 g) penne pasta
½ cup (60 g) pepperoni, quartered
24 oz (679 g) tomato sauce
8 oz (226 g) shredded Italian five cheese blend

Add the water, penne, pepperoni and tomato sauce to the Instant Pot insert without stirring. Seal the lid and turn the valve to the sealing position. Cook on manual, high pressure for 2 minutes. Release the pressure manually by carefully moving the valve to venting. Add the cheese blend and stir to combine.

LEMON-AVOCADO PIZZA PASTA CASSEROLE

1 lb (454 g) penne pasta
3 cups (720 ml) water
24 oz (680 g) tomato sauce
8 oz (226 g) shredded Italian five cheese blend
Zest of 1 lemon
1 avocado, pitted and diced
6 basil leaves, sliced into chiffonade (see Note on page 44)

Add the penne, water and tomato sauce to the Instant Pot insert without stirring. Seal the lid and turn the valve to the sealing position. Cook on manual, high pressure for 2 minutes. Release the pressure manually by carefully moving the valve to venting. Add the cheese blend and stir to combine. Top with lemon zest, avocado and basil.

BBQ CHICKEN PIZZA PASTA CASSEROLE

2 tbsp (28 g) unsalted butter
½ cup (57 g) red onion, sliced thinly
1 lb (454 g) penne pasta
3 cups (720 ml) water
1 cup (240 ml) BBQ sauce of choice
2 cups (250 g) rotisserie chicken
8 oz (226 g) shredded Italian five cheese blend
2 tsp (1 g) cilantro, roughly chopped

Turn the Instant Pot on to sauté mode. Add the butter and onion and sauté for 5 minutes. Add the penne and top with water, BBQ sauce and chicken, stirring to combine. Seal the lid and turn the valve to the sealing position. Cook on manual, high pressure for 2 minutes. Release the pressure manually by carefully moving the valve to venting. Add the cheese blend and cilantro and stir to combine.

CHICKEN PARMESAN BAKE

YIELD: 4 SERVINGS

If you love chicken Parmesan in the oven, you will love this Instant Pot version even more. It's conveniently made with chicken tenders, so no need for messy dredging or frying.

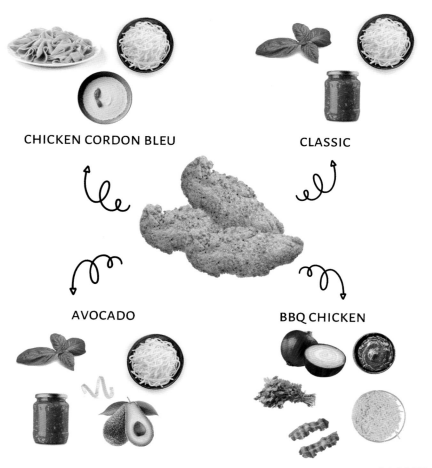

CHICKEN CORDON BLEU

CLASSIC

AVOCADO

BBQ CHICKEN

CLASSIC CHICKEN PARMESAN BAKE

4 frozen, pre-breaded chicken tenders
1 cup (240 ml) pasta sauce
1 cup (112 g) shredded Italian five cheese blend
1 cup (240 ml) water
4 basil leaves, sliced into chiffonade (see Note on page 44)

Place the chicken in an 8-inch (20-cm) cake pan, or other pan that fits your Instant Pot insert. Top with the pasta sauce and cheese blend. Cover the cake pan with a paper towel and then cover with foil. Pour the water into the bottom of the insert. Add the trivet and then the cake pan. Seal the lid and turn the valve to the sealing position. Cook on manual, high pressure for 25 minutes. Release the pressure manually by carefully moving the valve to venting. Remove the paper towel and foil and place the cake pan under the broiler to brown the cheese, about 3 minutes. Top with the basil.

NOTE

This dish is great to serve with pasta. You can even cook the pasta in the Instant Pot by cooking 8 ounces (226 g) of spaghetti with 2 cups (480 ml) of water on manual, high pressure for 8 minutes.

AVOCADO CHICKEN PARMESAN

4 frozen, pre-breaded chicken tenders
1 cup (240 ml) pasta sauce
1 cup (112 g) shredded Italian five cheese blend
1 cup (240 ml) water
4 basil leaves, sliced into chiffonade (see Note on page 44)
1 large avocado, pitted, skin removed and sliced
Zest of 1 lemon

Place the chicken in an 8-inch (20-cm) cake pan, or other pan that fits your Instant Pot insert. Top with the pasta sauce and cheese blend. Cover the cake pan with a paper towel and then cover with foil. Pour the water into the bottom of the insert. Add the trivet and then the cake pan. Seal the lid and turn the valve to the sealing position. Cook on manual, high pressure for 25 minutes. Release the pressure manually by carefully moving the valve to venting. Remove the paper towel and foil and place the cake pan under the broiler to brown the cheese, about 3 minutes. Top with the basil, avocado and lemon zest.

BBQ CHICKEN PARMESAN

1 tsp avocado or olive oil
¼ cup (29 g) red onion, sliced thinly
4 frozen, pre-breaded chicken tenders
1 cup (240 ml) BBQ sauce of choice
1 cup (113 g) shredded cheddar cheese
4 slices bacon, cooked until crispy and roughly chopped
1 tsp cilantro, roughly chopped

Turn the Instant Pot on to sauté mode. Add the oil and onion and sauté for 10 minutes, moving it around frequently to prevent burning. Remove the onion and set aside. Place the chicken in an 8-inch (20-cm) cake pan, or other pan that fits your Instant Pot insert. Top with the BBQ sauce, cheddar cheese, bacon and onion. Cover the cake pan with a paper towel and then cover with foil. Pour 1 cup (240 ml) of water into the bottom of the insert. Add the trivet and then the cake pan. Seal the lid and turn the valve to the sealing position. Cook on manual, high pressure for 25 minutes. Release the pressure manually by carefully moving the valve to venting. Remove the paper towel and foil and place the cake pan under the broiler to brown the cheese, about 3 minutes. Top with the cilantro.

CHICKEN CORDON BLEU PARMESAN

4 frozen, pre-breaded chicken tenders
4 thin slices of deli ham
1 cup (240 ml) premade alfredo sauce
1 cup (112 g) shredded Italian five cheese blend

Place the chicken in an 8-inch (20-cm) cake pan, or other pan that fits your Instant Pot insert. Top with the ham, alfredo sauce and cheese blend. Cover the cake pan with a paper towel and then cover with foil. Pour 1 cup (240 ml) of water into the bottom of the Instant Pot insert. Add the trivet and then the cake pan. Seal the lid and turn the valve to the sealing position. Cook on manual, high pressure for 25 minutes. Release the pressure manually by carefully moving the valve to venting. Remove the paper towel and foil and place the cake pan under the broiler to brown the cheese, about 3 minutes.

See image on page 106.

ENCHILADAS

YIELD: 6 ENCHILADAS

These enchiladas are full of melty cheese and delicious flavors.
I love adding vegetables like shredded zucchini to them. Try out the
Zucchini-Chicken Enchiladas (page 113) for a quick, healthy dinner option.
These enchiladas go fabulously with Mexican Beans (page 202) or with
Mexican Rice (page 194).

CREAMY CHICKEN

ZUCCHINI-CHICKEN

MUSHROOM TACO

CARNITAS

CREAMY CHICKEN ENCHILADAS

2 cups (226 g) pepper Jack cheese, shredded, divided
1 cup (125 g) rotisserie chicken, shredded
1 (10-oz [283-g]) can green mild enchilada sauce, divided
6 corn tortillas
Diced avocado, for serving (optional)
Diced tomatoes, for serving (optional)

In a small mixing bowl combine 1½ cups (170 g) of the pepper Jack cheese with the chicken. Pour about half the can of enchilada sauce into the bottom of an 8-inch (20-cm) cake pan, or other pan that fits your insert. Dip the tortillas into the sauce in the pan and fill each tortilla with ¼ cup (30 g) of the chicken mixture. Roll the tortilla up to form an enchilada. Repeat with the remaining tortillas.

Top the enchiladas with the remaining ½ cup (56 g) of pepper Jack cheese and remaining enchilada sauce and cover with foil. Add 1 cup (240 ml) of water to the Instant Pot and add the trivet. Place the cake pan on top of the trivet. Seal the lid and turn the valve to the sealing position. Cook on manual, high pressure for 10 minutes. Manually release the pressure by carefully moving the valve to venting. Remove the enchiladas and let them sit for 5 minutes before serving. Top them with the optional toppings.

CARNITAS ENCHILADAS

2 cups (226 g) pepper Jack cheese, shredded, divided
1 cup (134 g) pre-cooked carnitas, shredded
1 (10-oz [283-g]) can green mild enchilada sauce, divided
6 corn tortillas
Diced avocado, for serving (optional)
Diced white onion, for serving (optional)
Chopped cilantro, for serving (optional)

In a small mixing bowl combine 1½ cups (170 g) of pepper Jack cheese with the carnitas. Pour about half the can of enchilada sauce in the bottom of an 8-inch (20-cm) cake pan, or other pan that fits your insert. Dip the tortillas into the sauce in the pan and fill each tortilla with ¼ cup (30 g) of the carnitas mixture. Roll the tortillas up to form an enchilada. Repeat with the remaining tortillas.

Top the enchiladas with the remaining ½ cup (56 g) of pepper Jack cheese and remaining enchilada sauce and cover with foil. Add 1 cup (240 ml) of water to the Instant Pot and add the trivet. Place the cake pan on top of the trivet. Seal the lid and turn the valve to the sealing position. Cook on manual, high pressure for 10 minutes. Manually release the pressure by carefully moving the valve to venting. Remove the enchiladas and let them sit for 5 minutes before serving. Top with the optional toppings.

*See image on page 110.

ZUCCHINI-CHICKEN ENCHILADAS

2 cups (226 g) pepper Jack cheese, shredded, divided
1 cup (124 g) zucchini, finely shredded and drained
1 cup (125 g) rotisserie chicken, shredded
1 (10-oz [283-g]) can mild green enchilada sauce
6 corn tortillas
Diced avocado, for serving (optional)
Diced tomatoes, for serving (optional)

In a small mixing bowl combine 1½ cups (175 g) of the pepper Jack cheese with the zucchini and chicken. Pour about half the can of enchilada sauce in the bottom of an 8-inch (20-cm) cake pan or other pan that fits your insert. Dip the tortillas into the sauce in the pan and fill each tortilla with ¼ cup (30 g) of the chicken mixture. Roll the tortillas up to form an enchilada. Repeat with the remaining tortillas.

Top the enchiladas with the remaining ½ cup (56 g) of pepper Jack cheese and remaining enchilada sauce and cover with foil. Add 1 cup (240 ml) of water to the Instant Pot and add the trivet. Place the cake pan on top of the trivet. Seal the lid and turn the valve to the sealing position. Cook on manual, high pressure for 10 minutes. Manually release the pressure by carefully moving the valve to venting. Remove the enchiladas and let them sit for 5 minutes before serving. Top with the optional toppings.

MUSHROOM TACO ENCHILADAS

1 tsp avocado or olive oil
1 lb (454 g) button mushrooms, minced small
2 tsp (7 g) taco seasoning
Kosher salt, to taste
2 cups (226 g) pepper Jack cheese, shredded, divided
1 (10-oz [283-g]) can mild green enchilada sauce
6 corn tortillas
Diced avocado, for serving (optional)
Diced tomatoes, for serving (optional)

Turn the Instant Pot on to sauté mode. Add the oil and mushrooms and sauté for 5 to 7 minutes. Add the taco seasoning and salt and stir to combine. In a small mixing bowl combine the cooked mushroom mixture with 1½ cups (175 g) of the pepper Jack cheese. Pour about half the can of enchilada sauce in the bottom of an 8-inch (20-cm) cake pan, or other pan that fits your insert. Dip the tortillas into the sauce in the pan and fill each tortilla with ¼ cup (30 g) of the mushroom mixture. Roll the tortillas up to form an enchilada. Repeat with the remaining tortillas.

Top the enchiladas with the remaining ½ cup (56 g) of pepper Jack cheese and remaining enchilada sauce and cover with foil. Add 1 cup (240 ml) of water to the Instant Pot and add the trivet. Place the cake pan on top of the trivet. Seal the lid and turn the valve to the sealing position. Cook on manual, high pressure for 10 minutes. Manually release the pressure by carefully moving the valve to venting. Remove the enchiladas and let them sit for 5 minutes before serving. Top with the optional toppings.

LASAGNA

YIELD: 4 LARGE SERVINGS

Lasagna is the perfect casserole to make in the Instant Pot. I love to make an extra pan and freeze one for when I just don't feel like cooking.

CLASSIC

BUTTERNUT SQUASH

MUSHROOM AND KALE

MEXICAN

CLASSIC LASAGNA

1 lb (454 g) ground beef
1 lb (454 g) hot pork sausage, removed from casing
1 cup (240 ml) red cooking wine
1 (25-oz [708-g]) jar pasta sauce
1 (8-oz [226-g]) can tomato sauce
6 no-cook lasagna noodles
3 cups (336 g) shredded five cheese Italian blend
1 cup (246 g) ricotta cheese

Turn the Instant Pot on to sauté mode. Add the beef and sauté, breaking the meat into small pieces until browned and cooked through, about 7 minutes. Remove the beef and place in a mixing bowl. Add the sausage to the Instant Pot and sauté, breaking the meat into small pieces until browned and cooked through, about 7 minutes. Deglaze the pan with wine and scrape up any bits stuck to the bottom of the pan. Add the beef back into the insert along with the pasta and tomato sauces. Stir to combine and cook for 5 minutes.

Scoop ½ cup (120 ml) of the sauce into an 8-inch (20-cm) foil cake pan, or a pan that fits your Instant Pot. Top with a single layer of lasagna sheets. You may need to break the sheets up to fit the pan and to cover the surface area. Top with 1 cup (240 ml) of sauce and 1 cup (113 g) of shredded cheese blend. Add another layer of noodles. Evenly spread the ricotta cheese across the top and top with another layer of sauce, shredded cheese blend and noodles. Top with a final layer of sauce and shredded cheese blend and cover with foil.

Place 1 cup (240 ml) of water in the Instant Pot and add the trivet. Place the pan on top of the trivet. Seal the lid and turn the valve to the sealing position. Cook on manual, high pressure for 50 minutes. Release the pressure manually by carefully moving the valve to venting. Remove the lasagna and let it sit for 5 minutes before serving.

MUSHROOM AND KALE LASAGNA

2 tsp (10 ml) avocado or olive oil
2 lbs (907 g) mushrooms, sliced
2 cloves garlic, minced
4 cups (268 g) kale, ribs removed and sliced thinly
½ tsp kosher salt
1 cup (246 g) ricotta cheese
Zest of 1 lemon
1 (16-oz [454-g]) jar alfredo sauce
6 no-cook lasagna noodles
3 cups (336 g) shredded five cheese Italian blend

Turn the Instant Pot on to sauté mode. Add the oil, mushrooms and garlic and sauté for 5 minutes. Add the kale and cook for an additional 2 minutes to wilt. Remove the mushroom mixture and place in a mixing bowl. Combine the salt, ricotta cheese and lemon zest in a small bowl.

Pour ½ cup (120 ml) of the alfredo sauce into the bottom of an 8-inch (20-cm) foil cake pan or a pan that fits your Instant Pot. Top with a single layer of lasagna sheets. You may need to break the sheets up to fit the pan and to cover the surface area. Top with half of the mushroom and kale mixture. Sprinkle with 1 cup (113 g) of shredded cheese blend. Add another layer of noodles. Evenly spread the ricotta mixture across the top and top with the remaining mushroom mixture, another layer of sauce, cheese blend and noodles. Top with a final layer of sauce and cheese blend and cover with foil.

Add 1 cup (240 ml) of water into the Instant Pot and add the trivet. Place the pan on top of the trivet. Seal the lid and turn the valve to the sealing position. Cook on manual, high pressure for 50 minutes. Release the pressure manually by carefully moving the valve to venting. Remove the lasagna and let sit for 5 minutes before serving.

See image on page 114.

MEXICAN LASAGNA

1 lb (454 g) ground beef

2 cloves garlic, minced

2 tbsp (42 g) taco seasoning

1 (14.5-oz [411-g]) can diced tomatoes, drained

1 (12-oz [340-g]) jar mild red salsa

1 cup (154 g) frozen corn

6 no-cook lasagna noodles

3 cups (336 g) shredded cheddar cheese (see Note)

Turn the Instant Pot on to sauté mode. To make the sauce, add the ground beef and garlic and sauté, breaking the meat into small pieces until browned and cooked through, about 7 minutes. Remove the excess grease and add the taco seasoning. Add the tomatoes, salsa and corn and cook for 3 minutes.

Scoop out ½ cup (120 ml) of the sauce and place into an 8-inch (20-cm) foil cake pan or a pan that fits your Instant Pot. Top with a layer of lasagna sheets in one even layer; you may need to break the sheets up to fit the pan and to cover the surface area. Top with 1 cup (240 ml) of sauce and 1 cup (113 g) of cheddar cheese. Add another layer of noodles, sauce, cheese and noodles. Top with the remaining sauce and cheese and cover with foil.

Place 1 cup (240 ml) of water into the Instant Pot and add the trivet. Place the pan on top of the trivet. Seal the lid and turn the valve to the sealing position. Cook on manual, high pressure for 50 minutes. Release the pressure manually by carefully moving the valve to venting. Remove the lasagna and let it sit for 5 minutes before serving.

NOTE

I recommend grating a block of cheddar cheese, rather than using pre-shredded cheese for better melting. Pre-shredded cheese has anti-caking ingredients that make it harder to melt.

BUTTERNUT SQUASH LASAGNA

2 tbsp (28 g) unsalted butter

1 (15-oz [425-g]) container fresh butternut squash, diced

1 tsp kosher salt

1 tbsp (14 g) brown sugar

1 (15-oz [425-g]) container ricotta cheese

1 tsp fresh thyme, chopped

1 (16-oz [454-g]) jar alfredo sauce

6 no-cook lasagna noodles

3 cups (336 g) shredded five cheese Italian blend

Turn the Instant Pot on to sauté mode. Add the butter, squash, salt and brown sugar to the pot and cook for 15 minutes, stirring occasionally. Remove the squash mixture and place it in a food processor. Pulse until the squash is smooth but still has some texture to it, about 10 pulses. Combine the squash with the ricotta and thyme.

Pour ½ cup (120 ml) of the alfredo sauce in the bottom of an 8-inch (20-cm) foil cake pan or a pan that fits your Instant Pot. Top with a layer of lasagna sheets in one even layer. You may need to break the sheets up to fit the pan and to cover the surface area. Top with half of the butternut squash mixture. Sprinkle with 1 cup (113 g) of the shredded cheese blend. Add another layer of noodles. Evenly spread another layer of butternut squash, another layer of sauce, cheese blend and noodles. Top with a final layer of sauce and cheese blend and cover with foil.

Place 1 cup (240 ml) of water into the Instant Pot and add the trivet. Place the pan on top of the trivet. Seal the lid and turn the valve to the sealing position. Cook on manual, high pressure for 50 minutes. Release the pressure manually by carefully moving the valve to venting. Remove the lasagna and let it sit for 5 minutes before serving.

BREAKFAST

The Instant Pot is not just for dinner! The most important meal of the day can also be made quickly and easily in the Instant Pot. Most of these recipes can be made in advance and then frozen or prepped ahead to make breakfast time run effortlessly.

Make sure you try the Easy Mini Muffins (page 121)! They are a fan favorite at our house and can be changed up in so many different ways. My favorite variation is the Orange-Cranberry (page 122).

EASY MINI MUFFINS

YIELD: 24 MUFFINS

Mini muffins are perfect for a quick, make-ahead breakfast.
I make a big batch of these and keep them in a storage container to eat
throughout the week. You can even place them in a resealable bag and freeze
them for a freezer breakfast meal. Just pop them in the microwave
to reheat for a breakfast on the run.

MINT CHOCOLATE CHIP

BLUEBERRY

RASPBERRY-LEMON

ORANGE-CRANBERRY

ORANGE-CRANBERRY MINI MUFFINS

½ cup (100 g) granulated sugar
¼ cup (55 g) brown sugar
½ cup (114 g) unsalted butter, softened
2 eggs
½ cup (140 g) dry vanilla pudding mix
½ cup (120 ml) whole milk
1½ cups (188 g) all-purpose flour
2 tsp (9 g) baking powder
1 tsp kosher salt
½ cup (61 g) dried cranberries, rehydrated in hot water for 10 minutes
Zest of 1 orange
1 tbsp (15 ml) orange juice

Combine the sugars and butter in a stand mixer fitted with a paddle attachment and mix on low speed until creamy. Add the eggs and mix to combine. Add the pudding mix and mix to combine, scraping down the sides of the bowl occasionally. Add the milk, flour, baking powder and salt in that order and mix to combine. Drain the cranberries and add them to the mixer along with the orange zest and juice. Stir by hand to combine.

Spray an Instant Pot silicone mini muffin mold with cooking spray and place 1 tablespoon (15 ml) of batter into each muffin mold. Add 1 cup (240 ml) of water into the bottom of your Instant Pot insert. Add the trivet and top with the silicone mold.

Seal the lid and turn the valve to the sealing position. Turn the pot on manual, high pressure for 12 minutes. Release the pressure manually by carefully moving the valve to venting. Remove the silicone mold and let it cool for 5 minutes before inverting the muffins.

See image on page 120.

RASPBERRY-LEMON MINI MUFFINS

½ cup (100 g) granulated sugar
¼ cup (55 g) brown sugar
½ cup (114 g) unsalted butter, softened
2 eggs
½ cup (140 g) dry lemon pudding mix
½ cup (120 ml) whole milk
1½ cups (188 g) all-purpose flour
2 tsp (9 g) baking powder
1 tsp kosher salt
½ cup (63 g) fresh raspberries

Combine the sugars and butter in a stand mixer fitted with a paddle attachment and mix on low speed until creamy. Add the eggs and mix to combine. Add the pudding mix and mix to combine, scraping down the sides of the bowl occasionally. Add the milk and then the flour, baking powder and salt and mix to combine. Add the fresh raspberries and stir by hand to combine.

Spray an Instant Pot silicone mini muffin mold with cooking spray and place 1 tablespoon (15 ml) of batter into each muffin mold. Add 1 cup (240 ml) of water into the bottom of your Instant Pot insert. Add the trivet and top with the silicone mold.

Seal the lid and turn the valve to the sealing position. Turn the pot on manual, high pressure for 12 minutes. Release the pressure manually by carefully moving the valve to venting. Remove the silicone mold and let it cool for 5 minutes before inverting the muffins.

BLUEBERRY MINI MUFFINS

½ cup (100 g) granulated sugar
¼ cup (55 g) brown sugar
½ cup (114 g) unsalted butter, softened
2 eggs
½ cup (140 g) dry vanilla pudding mix
½ cup (120 ml) whole milk
1½ cups (188 g) all-purpose flour
2 tsp (9 g) baking powder
1 tsp kosher salt
½ cup (148 g) fresh or frozen blueberries

Combine the sugars and butter in a stand mixer fitted with a paddle attachment and mix on low speed until creamy. Add the eggs and mix to combine. Add the pudding mix and mix to combine, scraping down the sides of the bowl occasionally. Add the milk, flour, baking powder and salt and mix to combine. Add the blueberries and stir by hand to combine.

Spray an Instant Pot silicone mini muffin mold with cooking spray and place 1 tablespoon (15 ml) of batter into each muffin mold. Add 1 cup (240 ml) of water into the bottom of your Instant Pot insert. Add the trivet and top with the silicone mold.

Seal the lid and turn the valve to the sealing position. Turn the pot on manual, high pressure for 12 minutes. Release the pressure manually by carefully moving the valve to venting. Remove the silicone mold and let it cool for 5 minutes before inverting the muffins.

MINT CHOCOLATE CHIP MINI MUFFINS

½ cup (100 g) granulated sugar
¼ cup (55 g) brown sugar
½ cup (114 g) unsalted butter, softened
2 eggs
½ cup (140 g) dry chocolate pudding mix
1 tsp mint extract
½ cup (120 ml) whole milk
1½ cups (188 g) all-purpose flour
2 tsp (9 g) baking powder
1 tsp kosher salt
½ cup (86 g) mini chocolate chips

Combine the sugars and butter in a stand mixer fitted with a paddle attachment and mix on low speed until creamy. Add the eggs and mix to combine. Add the pudding mix and mint extract and mix to combine, scraping down the sides of the bowl occasionally. Add the milk, flour, baking powder and salt and mix to combine. Add the mini chocolate chips and stir by hand to combine.

Spray an Instant Pot silicone mini muffin mold with cooking spray and place 1 tablespoon (15 ml) of batter into each muffin mold. Add 1 cup (240 ml) of water into the bottom of your Instant Pot insert. Add the trivet and top with the silicone mold.

Seal the lid and turn the valve to the sealing position. Turn the pot on manual, high pressure for 12 minutes. Release the pressure manually by carefully moving the valve to venting. Remove the silicone mold and let it cool for 5 minutes before inverting the muffins.

MINI EGG FRITTATAS

YIELD: 24 MINI FRITTATAS

Mini egg frittatas are perfect to prep ahead for a quick breakfast. I love eating these as they are, or placing one in an English muffin to make a quick breakfast sandwich. They are perfect for using up leftover roasted veggies from the night before or vegetables that are on the verge of expiration.

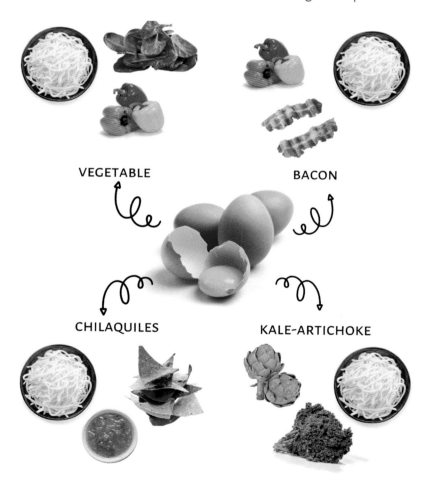

VEGETABLE

BACON

CHILAQUILES

KALE-ARTICHOKE

MINI BACON FRITTATAS

12 eggs

2 tbsp (30 ml) cream or whole milk

10 slices applewood smoked bacon, cooked until crispy and roughly chopped, about ⅔ cup (150 g)

⅓ cup (30 g) frozen bell pepper medley, roughly chopped (you may also use fresh)

1 cup (112 g) shredded Mozzarella cheese

½ tsp kosher salt

⅛ tsp black pepper

Crack the eggs into a blender with the cream and blend for 10 seconds. Transfer the egg mixture to a mixing bowl. Add the bacon, bell peppers, Mozzarella, salt and pepper and mix to combine. Fill a silicone egg bite mold two-thirds of the way full with the egg mixture. Add 1 cup (240 ml) of water to the bottom of the Instant Pot. Add the trivet and top with the silicone mold.

Seal the lid and turn the valve to the sealing position. Turn the pot on manual, high pressure for 12 minutes. Release the pressure manually by carefully moving the valve to venting. Remove the silicone mold and let it cool for 5 minutes before inverting the egg bites.

MINI VEGETABLE FRITTATAS

12 eggs

2 tbsp (30 ml) cream or whole milk

⅓ cup (30 g) frozen bell pepper medley, roughly chopped (you may also use fresh)

¼ cup (39 g) frozen spinach, thawed and drained

1 cup (112 g) shredded Mozzarella cheese

½ tsp kosher salt

⅛ tsp black pepper

Crack the eggs into a blender with the cream and blend for 10 seconds. Transfer the egg mixture to a mixing bowl. Add the bell peppers, spinach, Mozzarella, salt and pepper and mix to combine. Fill a silicone egg bite mold two-thirds of the way full with the egg mixture. Add 1 cup (240 ml) of water to the bottom of the Instant Pot. Add the trivet and top with the silicone mold.

Seal the lid and turn the valve to the sealing position. Turn the pot on manual, high pressure for 12 minutes. Release the pressure manually by carefully moving the valve to venting. Remove the silicone mold and let it cool for 5 minutes before inverting the egg bites.

MINI CHILAQUILES FRITTATAS

12 eggs

2 tbsp (30 ml) cream or whole milk

⅓ cup (80 ml) salsa verde

½ cup (13 g) corn tortilla chips, broken into small pieces

1 cup (112 g) shredded Mozzarella cheese

½ tsp kosher salt

⅛ tsp black pepper

2 tbsp (15 g) cotija cheese, crumbled

Hot sauce, to taste

Crack the eggs into a blender with the cream and blend for 10 seconds. Transfer the egg mixture to a mixing bowl. Add the salsa, chips, Mozzarella, salt and pepper and mix to combine. Fill a silicone egg bite mold two-thirds of the way full with the egg mixture. Add 1 cup (240 ml) of water to the bottom of the Instant Pot. Add the trivet and top with the silicone mold.

Seal the lid and turn the valve to the sealing position. Turn the pot on manual, high pressure for 12 minutes. Release the pressure manually by carefully moving the valve to venting. Remove the silicone mold and let it cool for 5 minutes before inverting the egg bites. Top the bites with cotija cheese and hot sauce.

MINI KALE-ARTICHOKE FRITTATAS

12 eggs

2 tbsp (30 ml) cream or whole milk

1 cup (67 g) kale, finely chopped

⅓ cup (87 g) canned artichoke hearts, drained, roughly chopped

1 cup (112 g) shredded Mozzarella cheese

½ tsp kosher salt

⅛ tsp black pepper

Crack the eggs into a blender with the cream and blend for 10 seconds. Transfer the egg mixture to a mixing bowl. Add the kale, artichokes, Mozzarella, salt and pepper and mix to combine. Fill a silicone egg bite mold two-thirds of the way full with the egg mixture. Add 1 cup (240 ml) of water to the bottom of the Instant Pot. Add the trivet and top with the silicone mold.

Seal the lid and turn the valve to the sealing position. Turn the pot on manual, high pressure for 12 minutes. Release the pressure manually by carefully moving the valve to venting. Remove the silicone mold and let it cool for 5 minutes before inverting the egg bites.

See image on page 124.

CROISSANT FRENCH TOAST CASSEROLE

YIELD: 6 SERVINGS

This delicious breakfast is an easy way to serve French toast without slaving over the stove. This is perfect for gatherings too. Just make the base and the toppings and let your guests decide what topping they prefer. It's a fun and delicious way to get your family involved.

PEANUT BUTTER AND JELLY

BANANA-CARAMEL

STRAWBERRIES AND CREAM

BLUEBERRY-MAPLE

PEANUT BUTTER AND JELLY CROISSANT FRENCH TOAST CASSEROLE

FOR THE FRENCH TOAST BASE

3 eggs

⅓ cup (66 g) granulated sugar

1 cup (240 ml) whole milk

1 tsp ground cinnamon

6 cups (250 g) day-old croissants, about 5 croissants, roughly torn into 1-inch (3-cm) chunks

FOR THE PEANUT BUTTER AND JELLY TOPPING

2 (14-oz [397-g]) cans sweetened condensed milk

½ cup (129 g) smooth peanut butter

2 tbsp (28 g) brown sugar

2 tbsp (30 ml) water

⅛ tsp almond emulsion (optional)

Pinch of salt

2 cups (246 g) raspberries

In a mixing bowl whisk together the eggs, sugar, milk and cinnamon. Add the croissants and stir to combine. Let the mixture sit for 5 minutes for the bread to soak up the custard. Spray a cake pan insert with cooking spray and pour the mixture into the pan. Cover with foil. Add 1 cup (240 ml) of water to the bottom of the Instant Pot insert. Add the trivet and top with the cake pan.

Seal the lid and turn the valve to the sealing position. Turn the Instant Pot on manual, high pressure for 40 minutes. Release the pressure manually by carefully moving the valve to venting. Remove the cake pan and foil.

Place all of the topping ingredients except the raspberries into a medium saucepan over medium heat. Stir and cook until warmed through and the peanut butter is completely melted. Slice the casserole into 6 equal servings. Top the French toast casserole with the peanut butter syrup and fresh raspberries.

BANANA-CARAMEL CROISSANT FRENCH TOAST CASSEROLE

FOR THE FRENCH TOAST BASE

3 eggs

⅓ cup (66 g) granulated sugar

1 cup (240 ml) whole milk

1 tsp ground cinnamon

6 cups (250 g) day-old croissants, about 5 croissants, roughly torn into 1-inch (3-cm) chunks

FOR THE BANANA-CARAMEL TOPPING

1 cup (200 g) granulated sugar

½ cup (120 ml) heavy cream

3 tbsp (42 g) unsalted butter

Pinch of kosher salt

1 tsp vanilla extract

3 ripe bananas, sliced

In a mixing bowl whisk together the eggs, sugar, milk and cinnamon. Add the croissants and stir to combine. Let the mixture sit for 5 minutes for the bread to soak up the custard. Spray a cake pan insert with cooking spray and pour the mixture into the pan. Cover with foil. Add 1 cup (240 ml) of water to the bottom of the Instant Pot insert. Add the trivet and top with the cake pan.

Seal the lid and turn the valve to the sealing position. Turn the Instant Pot on manual, high pressure for 40 minutes. Release the pressure manually by carefully moving the valve to venting. Remove the cake pan and foil.

Place the sugar in a medium-sized saucepan over medium heat. The sugar will start to melt. Stir it occasionally until it melts, about 5 minutes. Turn the heat up to medium high, stop stirring and cook the sugar until it becomes a light amber color, about 5 minutes. Remove the sugar from the heat and whisk in the heavy cream (the mixture will bubble up, so be careful). Whisk in the butter, salt and vanilla. Slice the casserole into 6 equal servings. Top the French toast casserole with the caramel syrup and banana slices.

STRAWBERRIES AND CREAM CROISSANT FRENCH TOAST CASSEROLE

FOR THE FRENCH TOAST BASE

3 eggs

⅓ cup (66 g) granulated sugar

1 cup (240 ml) whole milk

1 tsp ground cinnamon

6 cups (250 g) day-old croissants, about 5 croissants, roughly torn into 1-inch (3-cm) chunks

FOR THE STRAWBERRIES AND CREAM TOPPING

2 cups (280 g) frozen strawberries

½ cup (100 g) granulated sugar

¾ cup (180 ml) water

1 tsp vanilla extract

Whipped cream, for serving

In a mixing bowl whisk together the eggs, sugar, milk and cinnamon. Add the croissants and stir to combine. Let the mixture sit for 5 minutes for the bread to soak up the custard. Spray a cake pan insert with cooking spray and pour the mixture into the pan. Cover with foil. Add 1 cup (240 ml) of water to the bottom of the Instant Pot insert. Add the trivet and top with the cake pan.

Seal the lid and turn the valve to the sealing position. Turn the Instant Pot on manual, high pressure for 40 minutes. Release the pressure manually by carefully moving the valve to venting. Remove the cake pan and foil.

Combine the strawberries, sugar, water and vanilla in a small saucepan. Bring to a simmer and cook on medium-low heat for 7 minutes. Blend with an immersion blender or in a regular blender until smooth. Strain the mixture through a fine mesh strainer. Return to the pot to simmer just until thickened and the syrup can coat the back of a spoon, about 5 minutes. Slice the casserole into 6 equal servings. Top the French toast casserole with the strawberry syrup and whipped cream.

BLUEBERRY-MAPLE CROISSANT FRENCH TOAST CASSEROLE

FOR THE FRENCH TOAST BASE

3 eggs

⅓ cup (66 g) granulated sugar

1 cup (240 ml) whole milk

1 tsp ground cinnamon

6 cups (250 g) day-old croissants (about 5 croissants), roughly torn into 1-inch (3-cm) chunks

FOR THE BLUEBERRY-MAPLE TOPPING

2 oz (56 g) frozen blueberries

½ cup (120 ml) blueberry jam

¼ cup (50 g) granulated sugar

½ cup (120 ml) maple syrup

1 cup (240 ml) water

Pinch of salt

In a mixing bowl whisk together the eggs, sugar, milk and cinnamon. Add the croissants and stir to combine. Let the mixture sit for 5 minutes for the bread to soak up the custard. Spray a cake pan insert with cooking spray and pour the mixture into the pan. Cover with foil. Add 1 cup (240 ml) of water to the bottom of the Instant Pot insert. Add the trivet and top with the cake pan.

Seal the lid and turn the valve to the sealing position. Turn the Instant Pot on manual, high pressure for 40 minutes. Release the pressure manually by carefully moving the valve to venting. Remove the cake pan and foil.

Combine the blueberries, jam, sugar, maple syrup, water and salt in a small saucepan. Bring to a simmer and cook on medium-low heat for 12 minutes, or until thickened slightly. Blend with an immersion blender or in a regular blender until smooth. Strain the syrup through a fine mesh strainer. Slice the casserole into 6 equal servings. Top the French toast casserole with the blueberry syrup.

*See image on page 128.

COFFEE CAKE

YIELD: 8 SERVINGS

Sunday mornings call for this delicious, decadent coffee cake. Make sure you top it with one of these delicious toppings like the Banana-Toffee (page 134) variation. Also, the Instant Pot does wonders for coffee cake! It comes out moist and tender every time. The oven can cook coffee cake unevenly and often dries it out.

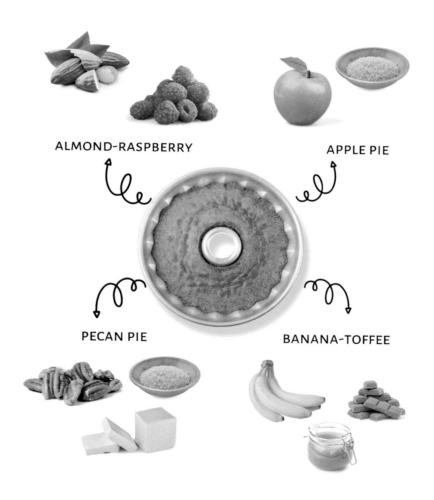

ALMOND-RASPBERRY

APPLE PIE

PECAN PIE

BANANA-TOFFEE

BANANA-TOFFEE COFFEE CAKE

FOR THE COFFEE CAKE BASE

2 cups (250 g) all-purpose flour

1 cup (200 g) granulated sugar

1 tsp kosher salt

½ cup plus 2 tbsp (142 g) unsalted butter, softened

1 tsp baking soda

1 tsp baking powder

¾ cup (180 ml) Greek yogurt

1 egg

¼ cup (60 ml) whole milk

1 tsp vanilla extract

FOR THE CRUMB TOPPING

½ cup (110 g) brown sugar

1 tsp ground cinnamon

FOR THE BANANA-TOFFEE TOPPING

4 bananas, sliced

2 (1.4-oz [39-g]) toffee candy bars, roughly chopped

¼ cup (60 ml) jarred caramel sauce, warmed

For the cake, in a medium bowl mix together the flour, sugar and salt. Cut in the butter, using a pastry cutter or two butter knives, until the mixture resembles coarse crumbs. Remove 1 cup of the crumbs and set aside. Add the baking soda, baking powder, yogurt, egg, milk and vanilla and stir until well combined.

Spray a springform pan that can fit the Instant Pot insert and fill it with the batter. For the crumb topping, add the brown sugar and cinnamon to the reserved crumbs. Sprinkle over the top of the cake and cover with a paper towel. Then cover with foil. Add 1 cup (240 ml) of water to the bottom of the Instant Pot insert. Add the trivet and top with the cake pan.

Seal the lid and turn the valve to the sealing position. Turn the Instant Pot on manual, high pressure for 45 minutes. Let the pressure release naturally for 5 minutes and then carefully move the valve to venting to release the rest of the pressure. Remove the cake pan and foil.

Top the coffee cake with the sliced bananas, toffee bits and a drizzle of caramel sauce and slice into 6 equal pieces.

ALMOND-RASPBERRY COFFEE CAKE

FOR THE COFFEE CAKE BASE

2 cups (250 g) all-purpose flour

1 cup (200 g) granulated sugar

1 tsp kosher salt

½ cup plus 2 tbsp (142 g) unsalted butter, softened

1 tsp baking soda

1 tsp baking powder

¾ cup (180 ml) Greek yogurt

1 egg

¼ cup (60 ml) whole milk

1 tsp almond emulsion

FOR THE CRUMB TOPPING

½ cup (110 g) brown sugar

1 tsp ground cinnamon

FOR THE ALMOND-RASPBERRY TOPPING

12 oz (340 g) fresh raspberries

1 tsp orange zest

1 tsp orange juice

¼ cup (30 g) sliced almonds, toasted

FOR THE GLAZE

½ cup (60 g) powdered sugar

1–2 tsp (5–10 ml) orange juice

Make the coffee cake base by following the instructions in the Banana-Toffee variation.

Spray a springform pan that can fit the Instant Pot insert and fill it with the batter. For the crumb topping, add the brown sugar and cinnamon to the reserved crumbs. Sprinkle over the top of the cake and cover with a paper towel, then foil. Add 1 cup (240 ml) of water to the bottom of the Instant Pot insert. Add the trivet and top with the cake pan.

Seal the lid and turn the valve to the sealing position. Turn the Instant Pot on manual, high pressure for 45 minutes. Let the pressure release naturally for 5 minutes and then carefully move the valve to venting to release the rest of the pressure. Remove the cake pan and foil.

For the raspberry topping and glaze, combine the raspberries, orange zest and juice in a small bowl and toss to combine. In another small bowl combine the powdered sugar and orange juice to create a thin glaze. Top the coffee cake with the raspberries and the toasted almonds, drizzle with the glaze and slice into 6 equal pieces.

PECAN PIE COFFEE CAKE

FOR THE COFFEE CAKE BASE

2 cups (250 g) all-purpose flour

1 cup (200 g) granulated sugar

1 tsp kosher salt

½ cup plus 2 tbsp (142 g) unsalted butter, softened

1 tsp baking soda

1 tsp baking powder

¾ cup (180 ml) Greek yogurt

1 egg

¼ cup (60 ml) whole milk

1 tsp vanilla extract

FOR THE CRUMB TOPPING

½ cup (110 g) brown sugar

1 tsp ground cinnamon

FOR THE PECAN PIE TOPPING

3 tbsp (42 g) unsalted butter

6 oz (168 g) pecan halves

½ cup (110 g) brown sugar

¼ cup (60 ml) corn syrup

Pinch of salt

Make the coffee cake base by following the instructions in the Banana-Toffee variation (page 134).

Spray a springform pan that can fit the Instant Pot insert and fill it with the batter. For the crumb topping, add the brown sugar and cinnamon to the reserved crumbs. Sprinkle it over the top of the cake and cover with a paper towel. Then cover with foil. Add 1 cup (240 ml) of water to the bottom of the Instant Pot insert. Add the trivet and top with the cake pan.

Seal the lid and turn the valve to the sealing position. Turn the Instant Pot on manual, high pressure for 45 minutes. Let the pressure release naturally for 5 minutes and then carefully move the valve to venting to release the rest of the pressure. Remove the cake pan and foil.

Place the butter, pecans, brown sugar, corn syrup and salt in a small saucepan over medium-low heat. Cook for 5 minutes, stirring frequently. Remove from the heat, top the coffee cake with the pecan topping and slice into 6 equal pieces.

See image on page 132.

APPLE PIE COFFEE CAKE

FOR THE COFFEE CAKE BASE

2 cups (250 g) all-purpose flour

1 cup (200 g) granulated sugar

1 tsp kosher salt

½ cup plus 2 tbsp (142 g) unsalted butter, softened

1 tsp baking soda

1 tsp baking powder

¾ cup (180 ml) Greek yogurt

1 egg

¼ cup (60 ml) whole milk

1 tsp vanilla extract

FOR THE CRUMB TOPPING

½ cup (110 g) brown sugar

1 tsp ground cinnamon

FOR THE APPLE PIE TOPPING

3 cups (360 g) Granny Smith apples, peeled and cored, sliced into ¼-inch (6-mm) slices

3 tbsp (42 g) unsalted butter

½ cup (110 g) brown sugar

2 tsp (5 g) cornstarch mixed with 1 tbsp (15 ml) cold water

¼ tsp ground cinnamon

Make the coffee cake base by following the instructions in the Banana-Toffee variation (page 134).

Spray a springform pan that can fit the Instant Pot insert and fill it with the batter. For the crumb topping, add the brown sugar and cinnamon to the reserved crumbs. Sprinkle it over the top of the cake and cover with a paper towel. Then cover with foil. Add 1 cup (240 ml) of water to the bottom of the Instant Pot insert. Add the trivet and top with the cake pan.

Seal the lid and turn the valve to the sealing position. Turn the Instant Pot on manual, high pressure for 45 minutes. Let the pressure release naturally for 5 minutes and then carefully move the valve to venting to release the rest of the pressure. Remove the cake pan and foil.

Place the apples, butter and brown sugar in a sauté pan over medium-low heat. Cook for 10 minutes, stirring frequently. Add the cornstarch mixture and cinnamon and stir to combine. Bring to a simmer to thicken and remove from the heat. Top the coffee cake with the apple topping and slice into 6 equal pieces.

CREAM CHEESE-FILLED BAGEL BITES

YIELD: 14 BAGEL BITES

These bagel bites are so insanely easy and can be transformed into any bagel and cream cheese combination you like. My favorite is the Everything Bagel Bites with Cream Cheese (page 138). You can find everything bagel seasoning at most major grocery stores in the spice aisle.

EVERYTHING

CINNAMON-PUMPKIN

JALAPEÑO-CHEDDAR

SESAME-BLUEBERRY

EVERYTHING BAGEL BITES WITH CREAM CHEESE

All-purpose flour for dusting
1 lb (454 g) pre-made pizza dough, divided
2 oz (56 g) cream cheese, divided
3 tbsp (42 g) unsalted butter, melted
Everything bagel blend seasoning, to taste

Dust a clean work surface with some flour and spray two silicone mini muffin molds with cooking spray. Place the pizza dough on the floured surface to prevent sticking. Grab about a golf ball–sized amount of dough and form a flat disk. Add 1 teaspoon of the cream cheese in the middle of the disk and then fold the edges together to form a ball. Roll gently to make sure the ball is sealed completely. Place the dough ball into the muffin mold. Repeat with the remaining dough and cream cheese.

Add 1 cup (240 ml) of water into the bottom of the Instant Pot. Add the trivet and then the silicone mold. Seal the lid and turn the valve to the sealing position. Turn the pot on manual, high pressure for 13 minutes. Release the pressure manually by carefully moving the valve to venting, then remove the silicone mold.

Let the bagel bites cool while you preheat the oven to 400°F (204°C). Remove the bagel bites from the mold and roll them in the melted butter. Place the bites on a foil-lined baking sheet and sprinkle generously with everything seasoning. Bake for 5 minutes to toast.

See image on page 136.

CINNAMON-SUGAR BAGEL BITES WITH PUMPKIN CREAM CHEESE

All-purpose flour for dusting
1 lb (454 g) pre-made pizza dough, divided
2 oz (60 g) pumpkin cream cheese, divided
½ cup (100 g) granulated sugar
1 tsp ground cinnamon
3 tbsp (42 g) unsalted butter, melted

Dust a clean work surface with some flour and spray two silicone mini muffin molds with cooking spray. Place the pizza dough on the floured surface to prevent sticking. Grab about a golf ball–sized amount of dough and form a flat disk. Add 1 teaspoon of the pumpkin cream cheese in the middle of the disk and then fold the edges together to form a ball. Roll gently to make sure the ball is sealed completely. Place the dough ball into the muffin mold. Repeat with the remaining dough and cream cheese.

Add 1 cup (240 ml) of water into the bottom of the Instant Pot. Add the trivet and then the silicone mold. Seal the lid and turn the valve to the sealing position. Turn the pot on manual, high pressure for 13 minutes. Release the pressure manually by carefully moving the valve to venting, then remove the silicone mold.

Let the bagel bites cool while you preheat the oven to 400°F (204°C). Combine the sugar with the cinnamon in a small bowl. Remove the bagel bites from the mold and roll them in the melted butter, then roll them in the cinnamon-sugar mixture. Bake the bites for 5 minutes to toast.

SESAME BAGEL BITES WITH BLUEBERRY CREAM CHEESE

All-purpose flour for dusting
1 lb (454 g) pre-made pizza dough, divided
2 oz (60 g) blueberry cream cheese, divided
3 tbsp (42 g) unsalted butter, melted
Sesame seeds, for garnish

Dust a clean work surface with some flour and spray two silicone mini muffin molds with cooking spray. Place the pizza dough on the floured surface to prevent sticking. Grab about a golf ball–sized amount of dough and form a flat disk. Add 1 teaspoon of the blueberry cream cheese in the middle of the disk and then fold the edges together to form a ball. Roll gently to make sure the ball is sealed completely. Place the dough ball into the muffin mold. Repeat with the remaining dough and cream cheese.

Add 1 cup (240 ml) of water into the bottom of the Instant Pot. Add the trivet and then the silicone mold. Seal the lid and turn the valve to the sealing position. Turn the pot on manual, high pressure for 13 minutes. Release the pressure manually by carefully moving the valve to venting, then remove the silicone mold.

Let the bagel bites cool while you preheat the oven to 400°F (204°C). Remove the bagel bites from the mold and roll them in the melted butter. Place on a foil-lined baking sheet and sprinkle generously with sesame seeds. Bake the bites for 5 minutes to toast.

CHEDDAR BAGEL BITES WITH JALAPEÑO CREAM CHEESE

All-purpose flour for dusting
1 lb (454 g) pre-made pizza dough, divided
2 oz (60 g) jalapeño cream cheese, divided
3 tbsp (42 g) unsalted butter, melted
½ cup (57 g) shredded cheddar cheese

Dust a clean work surface with some flour and spray two silicone mini muffin molds with cooking spray. Place the pizza dough on the floured surface to prevent sticking. Grab about a golf ball–sized amount of dough and form a flat disk. Add 1 teaspoon of jalapeño cream cheese in the middle of the disk and then fold the edges together to form a ball. Roll gently to make sure the ball is sealed completely. Place the dough ball into the muffin mold. Repeat with the remaining dough and cream cheese.

Add 1 cup (240 ml) of water into the bottom of the Instant Pot. Add the trivet and then the silicone mold. Seal the lid and turn the valve to the sealing position. Turn the pot on manual, high pressure for 13 minutes. Release the pressure manually by carefully moving the valve to venting, then remove the silicone mold.

Let the bagel bites cool while you preheat the oven to 400°F (204°C). Remove the bagel bites from the mold and roll them in the melted butter. Place on a foil-lined baking sheet and sprinkle generously with the cheddar cheese. Bake for 5 minutes to toast.

SWEET ROLLS

YIELD: 24 SMALL ROLLS OR 16 LARGE ROLLS

Cinnamon rolls are a tradition in our home for special occasions. We make these rolls for Christmas, birthdays and Easter. I love a good traditional cinnamon roll, but these flavor combinations will blow your mind! They are fun, exciting and will awaken your taste buds.

ALMOND

PEANUT BUTTER AND JELLY

CHOCOLATE-STRAWBERRY

ORANGE

ORANGE SWEET ROLLS

FOR THE ROLLS

1¾ cups (420 ml) warm water

3 tbsp (36 g) dry active yeast

½ cup (120 ml) vegetable oil

½ cup (100 g) granulated sugar

2 eggs

1½ tsp (9 g) kosher salt

5¼–5½ cups (710–754 g) bread flour

FOR THE FILLING

½ cup (100 g) granulated sugar

Zest of 3 large oranges

½ cup (114 g) unsalted butter, softened

FOR THE FROSTING

½ cup (114 g) unsalted butter, at room temperature

8 oz (226 g) cream cheese, at room temperature

4 cups (480 g) powdered sugar

Zest of 2 oranges

Prepare a cake pan insert with cooking spray. In an electric mixer fitted with a dough hook, combine the water, yeast, oil and sugar. Let it sit for 10 minutes. Add the eggs, salt and flour and mix on low speed for 2 minutes until the dough is combined and pulls off the sides.

Smear extra oil onto a clean counter and press the dough out into a 9 x 13–inch (23 x 33–cm) rectangle. For the filling, combine the sugar, orange zest and butter in a small bowl. Spread the filling evenly over the dough. Starting on the long end closest to you, roll the dough tightly into a long log. Using a bench scraper, cut the log into 16 large rolls or 24 small rolls. Place 6 rolls into the prepared cake pan and cover with a paper towel, then with foil.

Add 1 cup (240 ml) of water into the bottom of the Instant Pot. Add the trivet and then the cake pan. Seal the lid and turn the valve to the sealing position. Turn the pot on manual, high pressure for 23 minutes.

Make the frosting by combining the butter and cream cheese in a mixer fitted with a paddle attachment. Mix in the powdered sugar and orange zest. When the rolls are done, release the pressure manually by carefully moving the valve to venting. Frost the rolls while they are warm. Repeat the cooking and frosting process for the remaining rolls.

ALMOND SWEET ROLLS

FOR THE ROLLS

1¾ cups (420 ml) warm water

3 tbsp (36 g) dry active yeast

½ cup (120 ml) vegetable oil

½ cup (100 g) granulated sugar

2 eggs

1½ tsp (9 g) kosher salt

5¼–5½ cups (710–754 g) bread flour

FOR THE FILLING

½ cup (114 g) unsalted butter, softened

½ cup (100 g) granulated sugar

14 oz (396 g) almond paste

FOR THE FROSTING

½ cup (114 g) unsalted butter, at room temperature

8 oz (226 g) cream cheese, at room temperature

4 cups (480 g) powdered sugar

1 tsp almond extract

Make the dough by following the instructions in the Orange Rolls variation.

Smear extra oil onto a clean counter and press the dough out into a 9 x 13–inch (23 x 33–cm) rectangle with the long side closest to you. For the filling, spread the butter on the dough with a spatula. Sprinkle the buttered dough with the sugar and then evenly distribute the almond paste across the whole surface of the dough by crumbling it into little pieces. Starting on the end closest to you, roll and pinch the dough to form a seam, then roll the dough tightly into a long log. Using a bench scraper, cut the log into 16 large rolls or 24 small rolls. Place 6 rolls into the prepared cake pan and cover with a paper towel, then with foil.

Add 1 cup (240 ml) of water into the bottom of the Instant Pot. Add the trivet and then the pan. Seal the lid and turn the valve to the sealing position. Turn the pot on manual, high pressure for 23 minutes.

Make the frosting by combining the butter and cream cheese in a mixer fitted with a paddle attachment. Mix in the sugar and almond extract. When the rolls are done, release the pressure manually by carefully moving the valve to venting. Frost the rolls while they are warm. Repeat the cooking and frosting process for the remaining rolls.

PEANUT BUTTER AND JELLY SWEET ROLLS

FOR THE ROLLS

1¾ cups (420 ml) warm water

3 tbsp (36 g) dry active yeast

½ cup (120 ml) vegetable oil

½ cup (100 g) granulated sugar

2 eggs

1½ tsp (9 g) kosher salt

5¼–5½ cups (710–754 g) bread flour

FOR THE FILLING

1 cup (240 ml) boysenberry jam

½ cup (100 g) granulated sugar

½ cup (114 g) unsalted butter, softened

1 tsp ground cinnamon

FOR THE FROSTING

½ cup (114 g) unsalted butter, at room temperature

8 oz (226 g) cream cheese, at room temperature

4 cups (480 g) powdered sugar

½ tsp almond emulsion

⅓ cup (86 g) chunky peanut butter

Make the dough by following the instructions in the Orange Rolls variation (page 142).

Smear extra oil onto a clean counter and press the dough out into a 9 x 13–inch (23 x 33–cm) rectangle with the long side closest to you. For the filling, combine the jam, sugar, butter and cinnamon in a small bowl. Spread the filling evenly over the dough. Starting on the long end closest to you, roll and pinch the dough to form a seam, then roll the dough tightly into a long log. Using a bench scraper, cut the log into 16 large rolls or 24 small rolls. Place 6 rolls into the prepared cake pan and cover with a paper towel, then with foil.

Add 1 cup (240 ml) of water into the bottom of the Instant Pot. Add the trivet and then the cake pan. Seal the lid and turn the valve to the sealing position. Turn the pot on manual, high pressure for 23 minutes.

Make the frosting by combining the butter and cream cheese in a mixer fitted with a paddle attachment. Mix in the sugar, almond emulsion and peanut butter. When the rolls are done, release the pressure manually by carefully moving the valve to venting. Frost the rolls while they are warm. Repeat the cooking and frosting process for the remaining rolls.

CHOCOLATE-STRAWBERRY SWEET ROLLS

FOR THE ROLLS

2 cups (480 ml) warm water

3 tbsp (36 g) dry active yeast

½ cup (120 ml) vegetable oil

½ cup (100 g) granulated sugar

2 eggs

1½ tsp (9 g) kosher salt

2 tbsp (11 g) dark cocoa powder

5¼–5½ cups (710–754 g) bread flour

FOR THE FILLING

1 (3.9-oz [110-g]) box chocolate pudding mix

½ cup (114 g) unsalted butter, melted

FOR THE FROSTING

½ cup (114 g) unsalted butter, at room temperature

8 oz (226 g) cream cheese, at room temperature

4 cups (480 g) powdered sugar

¼ cup (42 g) strawberries, roughly chopped

Make the dough by following the instructions in the Orange Rolls variation (page 142), adding the cocoa before the flour.

Smear extra oil onto a clean counter and press the dough out into a 9 x 13–inch (23 x 33–cm) rectangle. For the filling, combine the pudding mix and butter in a small bowl. Spread the filling evenly over the dough. Starting on the long end closest to you, roll the dough tightly into a long log. Cut the log into 16 large rolls or 24 small rolls. Place 6 rolls into the prepared cake pan and cover with a paper towel, then with foil.

Add 1 cup (240 ml) of water into the bottom of the Instant Pot. Add the trivet and then the cake pan. Seal the lid and turn the valve to the sealing position. Turn the pot on manual, high pressure for 23 minutes.

Make the frosting by combining the butter and cream cheese in a mixer fitted with a paddle attachment. Mix in the powdered sugar and strawberries. When the rolls are done, release the pressure manually by carefully moving the valve to venting. Frost the rolls while they are still warm. Repeat the cooking and frosting process for the remaining rolls.

*See image on page 140.

SOFT-BOILED EGGS

YIELD: 2 SERVINGS

Soft-boiled eggs are one of my favorite breakfasts. My mom used to make them on toast for dinner sometimes, and they're a total comfort food for me. I love how easy they are to make in the Instant Pot and you will get the same delicious result every time.

CALIFORNIA

MEXICAN

CRAB BENEDICT

CREOLE BENEDICT

CALIFORNIA TOAST WITH SHAVED RADISH

4 eggs
4 slices sourdough bread, toasted
2 avocados, halved and pitted
2 tbsp (10 g) white onion, diced small
3 tbsp (45 ml) lemon juice, divided
1 tbsp (3 g) fresh dill, roughly chopped
½ tsp kosher salt
½ cup (58 g) radish, shaved

Add 1 cup (240 ml) of water to the bottom of the Instant Pot insert. Add the egg trivet and top with the eggs. Seal the lid and turn the valve to the sealing position. Turn the Instant Pot on manual, low pressure for 5 minutes. Release the pressure manually by carefully moving the valve to venting. Carefully remove the eggs and run them under cold water. Peel the eggs under cold running water.

Place the toasted bread on your serving plate. In a bowl, combine the avocados, onion, 1 tablespoon (15 ml) of the lemon juice, dill and salt and divide the mixture evenly among the toasted bread. Combine the radish and the remaining 2 tablespoons (30 ml) of the lemon juice and place on top of the avocados. Top with the soft-boiled eggs.

MEXICAN AVOCADO TOAST

4 eggs
4 slices sourdough bread, toasted
2 avocados, halved, pitted and sliced
½ cup (69 g) chorizo, cooked and crumbled
1 tbsp (8 g) cotija cheese
1 lime, juiced

Add 1 cup (240 ml) of water to the bottom of the Instant Pot insert. Add the egg trivet and top with the eggs. Seal the lid and turn the valve to the sealing position. Turn the Instant Pot on manual, low pressure for 5 minutes. Release the pressure manually by carefully moving the valve to venting. Carefully remove the eggs and run them under cold water. Peel the eggs under cold running water.

Place the toasted bread on your serving plate. Divide the avocados, chorizo, cotija cheese and lime juice evenly among the toasted bread. Top with the soft-boiled eggs.

CRAB BENEDICT

5 eggs, divided
½ tsp blackening seasoning
¼ cup (60 ml) mayonnaise
1 tbsp (4 g) parsley, finely chopped
Kosher salt, to taste
1 lb (454 g) jumbo lump crabmeat
¼ cup (14 g) panko bread crumbs, plus more for topping
3 tbsp (42 g) unsalted butter
4 slices sourdough bread, toasted

FOR THE HOLLANDAISE SAUCE

3 egg yolks and 1 whole egg (use pasteurized eggs)
Zest of 1 lemon
1 tbsp (15 ml) lemon juice
½ tsp kosher salt
½ cup (114 g) unsalted butter, melted and hot

Add 1 cup (240 ml) of water to the bottom of the Instant Pot insert. Add the egg trivet and top with 4 of the eggs. Seal the lid and turn the valve to the sealing position. Turn the Instant Pot on manual, low pressure for 5 minutes. Release the pressure manually by carefully moving the valve to venting. Carefully remove the eggs and run them under cold water. Peel the eggs under cold running water.

Combine the blackening seasoning, remaining egg, mayonnaise, parsley and salt in a mixing bowl and gently fold in the crab meat. Scoop ¼ cup (about 60 g) of the crab mixture and mold tightly into a cake (you should get 4 crab cakes). Refrigerate for at least 1 hour. When ready to cook, sprinkle one side of the crab cakes with the panko bread crumbs.

Preheat a nonstick sauté pan over medium heat and add the butter. Sauté the crab cakes, panko side down, in the butter for 3 to 5 minutes, or until golden brown. Sprinkle the tops with more panko and flip to cook the other side until golden brown.

Place the toasted bread on your serving plate. Prepare the hollandaise by placing the egg yolks and egg in a small blender, or use an immersion blender and a jar. Add the lemon zest and juice, salt and butter and immediately blend on high for 2 minutes. Top the toasted bread with the crab cakes, soft-boiled eggs and hollandaise.

CREOLE BENEDICT

4 eggs
1 tsp avocado or olive oil
6 oz (170 g) andouille sausage, sliced thinly
4 slices sourdough bread, toasted

FOR THE HOLLANDAISE SAUCE

3 egg yolks and 1 whole egg (use pasteurized eggs)
Zest of 1 lemon
1 tbsp (15 ml) lemon juice
½ tsp blackening seasoning
½ cup (114 g) unsalted butter, melted and hot
Kosher salt to taste

Add 1 cup (240 ml) of water to the bottom of the Instant Pot insert. Add the egg trivet and top with the eggs. Seal the lid and turn the valve to the sealing position. Turn the Instant Pot on manual, low pressure for 5 minutes. Release the pressure manually by carefully moving the valve to venting. Carefully remove the eggs and run them under cold water. Peel the eggs under cold running water.

Preheat a nonstick sauté pan over medium heat and add the oil and sausage. Sauté for 5 to 7 minutes, or until golden brown. Place the toasted bread on your serving plate.

Prepare the hollandaise by placing the egg yolks and egg in a small blender, or use an immersion blender and a jar. Add the lemon zest and juice, blackening seasoning, butter and salt to taste and immediately blend on high for 2 minutes. Top the toasted bread with the sausage, soft-boiled eggs and hollandaise.

See image on page 144.

EGG CASSEROLE

Egg casserole is a great meal prep item to make once a week to have on hand. You can store slices of the casserole in an airtight container for up to one week in the fridge. Just microwave a slice each morning for a quick hot breakfast.

VEGETABLE BRUSCHETTA

BACON AND CHEESE

SAUSAGE AND SPINACH

FIESTA

VEGETABLE BRUSCHETTA EGG CASSEROLE

8 eggs
½ cup (75 g) bell peppers, roughly chopped
1 cup (70 g) mushrooms, roughly chopped
1 cup (30 g) spinach, roughly chopped
½ cup (120 g) prepared bruschetta topping, drained slightly
1 cup (112 g) shredded Italian five cheese blend
Kosher salt and pepper to taste

Prepare a cake pan insert that will fit into your Instant Pot with cooking spray.

Place the eggs in a mixing bowl and whisk until scrambled. Add the bell peppers, mushrooms, spinach, bruschetta topping and cheese blend, and season with salt and pepper, then whisk to combine. Pour the egg mixture into the prepared pan. Cover with foil. Add 1 cup (240 ml) of water to the bottom of the Instant Pot insert. Add the trivet and top with the cake pan. Seal the lid and turn the valve to the sealing position. Turn the Instant Pot on manual, high pressure for 45 minutes. Release pressure manually by carefully moving the valve to venting. Remove the cake pan and foil. To serve, cut the casserole into 8 equal slices.

See image on page 148.

FIESTA EGG CASSEROLE

8 eggs
12 slices applewood smoked bacon, cooked until crispy and roughly chopped, about ¾ cup (169 g)
1 cup (149 g) bell peppers, diced
¼ cup (60 ml) red salsa
1 cup (113 g) shredded cheddar cheese
Kosher salt and pepper to taste

Prepare a cake pan insert that will fit into your Instant Pot with cooking spray.

Place the eggs in a mixing bowl and whisk until scrambled. Add the bacon, bell peppers, salsa and cheddar cheese and season with salt and pepper, then whisk to combine. Pour the egg mixture into the prepared pan. Cover with foil. Add 1 cup (240 ml) of water to the bottom of the Instant Pot insert. Add the trivet and top with the cake pan. Seal the lid and turn the valve to the sealing position. Turn the Instant Pot on manual, high pressure for 45 minutes. Release the pressure manually by carefully moving the valve to venting. Remove the cake pan and foil. To serve, cut the casserole into 8 equal slices.

SAUSAGE AND SPINACH EGG CASSEROLE

8 eggs
1 cup (156 g) frozen spinach, thawed and squeezed dry
1 cup (138 g) cooked sausage, roughly chopped
1 cup (113 g) pepper Jack cheese
Kosher salt and black pepper to taste

Prepare a cake pan insert that will fit into your Instant Pot with cooking spray.

Place the eggs in a mixing bowl and whisk until scrambled. Add the spinach, sausage and pepper Jack cheese and season with salt and pepper, whisking to combine. Pour the egg mixture into the prepared pan. Cover with foil. Add 1 cup (240 ml) of water to the bottom of the Instant Pot insert. Add the trivet and top with the cake pan. Seal the lid and turn the valve to the sealing position. Turn the Instant Pot on manual, high pressure for 45 minutes. Release the pressure manually by carefully moving the valve to venting. Remove the cake pan and foil. To serve, cut the casserole into 8 equal slices.

BACON AND CHEDDAR EGG CASSEROLE

8 eggs
12 slices applewood smoked bacon, cooked until crispy and roughly chopped, about ¾ cup (169 g)
¾ cup (63 g) frozen shredded hash browns
1 cup (113 g) shredded cheddar cheese
Kosher salt and pepper to taste

Prepare a cake pan insert that will fit into your Instant Pot with cooking spray.

Place the eggs in a mixing bowl and whisk until scrambled. Add the bacon, hash browns and cheddar cheese and season with salt and pepper, then whisk to combine. Pour the egg mixture into the prepared pan. Cover with foil. Add 1 cup (240 ml) of water to the bottom of the Instant Pot insert. Add the trivet and top with the cake pan. Seal the lid and turn the valve to the sealing position. Turn the Instant Pot on manual, high pressure for 45 minutes. Release the pressure manually by carefully moving the valve to venting. Remove the cake pan and foil. Slice the casserole into 8 equal slices and serve.

YOGURT

YIELD: 10 SERVINGS

Yogurt is great to make in the Instant Pot. It sounds a little tricky, but just follow the directions and you will have great yogurt every time. It is very important to buy yogurt, used as a starter, that reads "with live cultures" on the label. If you want a thicker yogurt, you can always let your yogurt drain through some cheesecloth in the fridge after it has incubated.

CARDAMOM

AÇAI

STRAWBERRY-MINT

LEMON–CHIA SEED

CARDAMOM YOGURT

8 cups (1.8 L) whole milk
2 tbsp (30 ml) yogurt "with live cultures"
½ cup (120 ml) sweetened condensed milk
1 tsp vanilla extract or vanilla bean paste

FOR THE CARDAMOM MIX-IN

1 tsp ground cardamom
1 tsp almond emulsion

Run the Instant Pot lid and insert through a heavy cycle in the dishwasher to sterilize. Add the milk to the Instant Pot insert and seal with the lid. Turn the valve to the venting position. Press the yogurt button until the pot reads boil. If you have an older model, you can turn on sauté mode for this part (just be sure to keep an eye on it so it doesn't boil over). It will cook for about 20 to 30 minutes. When it begins to beep, remove the lid and check the temperature of the milk with a digital thermometer. If it reads 185°F (85°C) or above, remove the insert and place it in a large bowl of ice water to lower the temperature to 115°F (46°C). This will take about 15 minutes. You don't want it to drop below 110°F (43°C).

Dry off the bottom of the pot and place the insert back into the Instant Pot. With a ladle, scoop 1 cup (240 ml) of the warm milk into a small mixing bowl. Add the yogurt, condensed milk and vanilla and stir to combine. Add the mixture back to the remaining milk in the Instant Pot. Place the lid back on and press the yogurt button until the pot reads 8:00. Do not move the valve to sealing—keep it at the venting position. Let the yogurt incubate for 8 hours. You can add an additional 2 hours if you want thicker yogurt. Try not to stir the yogurt. You can check thickness by sticking a spoon into the yogurt after 6 hours. When the yogurt is ready, remove the insert and let the yogurt rest for 1 hour at room temperature. Then place the insert in the fridge.

When the yogurt is done, stir in ground cardamom and almond emulsion.

AÇAI YOGURT

FOR THE BASE YOGURT

8 cups (1.8 L) whole milk
2 tbsp (30 ml) yogurt "with live cultures"
½ cup (120 ml) sweetened condensed milk
1 tsp vanilla extract or vanilla bean paste

FOR THE AÇAI MIX-IN

1 (3.5-oz [100-g]) packet frozen açai berries, thawed
Granola, for topping (optional)
Shredded coconut, for topping (optional)
Sliced bananas, for topping (optional)
Sliced strawberries, for topping (optional)
Honey, for topping (optional)

Make the base yogurt by following the instructions in the Cardamom variation.

When the yogurt is done, stir in the açai and your choice of granola, coconut, bananas, strawberries and honey (if using).

LEMON-CHIA SEED YOGURT

8 cups (1.8 L) whole milk

2 tbsp (30 ml) yogurt "with live cultures"

½ cup (120 ml) sweetened condensed milk

1 tsp vanilla extract or vanilla bean paste

FOR THE LEMON-CHIA SEED MIX-IN

2 tbsp (20 g) chia seeds

2 tbsp (30 ml) water

½ cup (120 ml) lemon curd

Make the base yogurt by following the instructions in the Cardamom variation (page 154).

Combine the chia seeds with the water and let the mixture sit for 2 minutes. Add the lemon curd and stir to combine. When the yogurt is done, stir in the lemon curd mixture.

See image on page 152.

STRAWBERRY-MINT YOGURT

FOR THE BASE YOGURT

8 cups (1.8 L) whole milk

2 tbsp (30 ml) yogurt "with live cultures"

½ cup (120 ml) sweetened condensed milk

1 tsp vanilla extract or vanilla bean paste

FOR THE STRAWBERRY-MINT MIX-IN

1 lb (454 g) strawberries, sliced in quarters

½ cup (100 g) granulated sugar

1 tbsp (6 g) mint, roughly chopped

Make the base yogurt by following the instructions in the Cardamom variation (page 154).

Combine the strawberries and sugar and let the mixture sit for 20 minutes. Add the mint and stir to combine. When the yogurt is done, stir the strawberry mixture into the yogurt or top individual servings.

APPETIZERS

What better way to start a party off than with some delicious appetizers!
The Instant Pot makes it effortless. You can even serve some of these dishes
straight from the Instant Pot for a one-pot meal.

One of my favorite appetizers to serve at a party is meatballs. Try out the
Jalapeño Popper Meatballs (page 160) for a great game day appetizer or tailgating
recipe. You can make them, keep them hot and serve them all in the Instant Pot. Just
turn the machine to the warming mode so your dishes stay warm all party long.

And don't forget the deviled eggs. We love serving them for an elegant Easter
appetizer. The Lox Deviled Eggs (page 169) are perfect to serve for brunch.

MEATBALLS

YIELD: 28 MEATBALLS

Meatballs are so versatile. I love filling them with different cheeses or peppers. You can change up the meat and use ground turkey or pork. Serve these unique meatballs at your next party or eat them for dinner on pasta or in a sub sandwich!

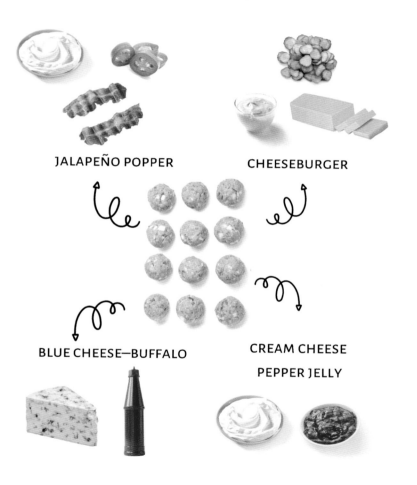

JALAPEÑO POPPER

CHEESEBURGER

BLUE CHEESE—BUFFALO

CREAM CHEESE

PEPPER JELLY

BLUE CHEESE-BUFFALO MEATBALLS

2 lbs (907 g) 80/20 ground beef

2 eggs

¼ cup (14 g) panko bread crumbs

1½ tsp (9 g) kosher salt

¼ cup (34 g) blue cheese crumbles

1 tbsp (15 ml) avocado or olive oil

Buffalo sauce, to taste

Ranch dressing, to taste

1 tsp Italian parsley, roughly chopped, for garnish

In a mixing bowl combine the beef, eggs, panko and salt. Be careful not to overmix. Scoop a golf ball–sized amount of meat mixture into your hand. Form a ball and press your finger into the middle to form an indent. Place a small blue cheese crumble into the indent. Press the meat mixture on top of the blue cheese to form a meatball and to seal the cheese inside. Repeat with the remaining meat mixture and blue cheese to form 28 meatballs total.

Turn the Instant Pot on to sauté mode and add the oil. Sauté the meatballs for about 5 minutes on all sides to brown. Be careful not to overcrowd the pan; you will need to do this in multiple batches. Remove the meatballs and place them in an oven-safe baking dish. I like to use an 8-inch (20-cm) cake pan.

Place 1½ cups (360 ml) of water in the bottom of your Instant Pot insert (no need to clean it) and add the trivet. Place the cake pan on the trivet and close the lid. Make sure the valve is turned to sealing. Cook on steam mode for 6 minutes. Manually release the pressure by carefully moving the valve to venting. Carefully remove the meatballs and place them in your serving bowl. Drizzle them with buffalo sauce and ranch dressing. Top with parsley.

JALAPEÑO POPPER MEATBALLS

2 lbs (907 g) 80/20 ground beef

2 eggs

¼ cup (14 g) panko bread crumbs

1½ tsp (9 g) kosher salt

¼ cup (30 g) cream cheese, cut into ¼-inch (6-mm) cubes

¼ cup (30 g) tamed pickled jalapeños

1 tbsp (15 ml) avocado or olive oil

3 slices bacon, cooked until crispy and roughly chopped, for garnish

In a mixing bowl combine the beef, eggs, panko and salt. Be careful not to overmix. Scoop a golf ball–sized amount of meat mixture into your hand. Form a ball and press your finger into the middle to form an indent. Place a cube of cream cheese and a tamed jalapeño into the indent. Press the meat mixture on top of the cream cheese to form a meatball and to seal the cheese and jalapeño inside. Make sure the filling is completely enclosed. Repeat with the remaining meat mixture, cream cheese and jalapeño to form 28 meatballs total.

Turn the Instant Pot on to sauté mode and add the oil. Sauté the meatballs for about 5 minutes on all sides to brown. Be careful not to overcrowd the pan, you will need to do this in multiple batches. Remove the meatballs and place them in an oven-safe baking dish. I like to use an 8-inch (20-cm) cake pan.

Place 1½ cups (360 ml) of water in the bottom of your Instant Pot insert, no need to clean it, and add the trivet. Place the cake pan on the trivet and close the lid. Make sure the valve is turned to sealing. Cook on steam mode for 6 minutes. Manually release the pressure by carefully moving the valve to venting. Carefully remove the meatballs and place them in your serving bowl. Top with the crispy bacon.

See image on page 158.

CREAM CHEESE PEPPER JELLY MEATBALLS

2 lbs (907 g) 80/20 ground beef
2 eggs
¼ cup (14 g) panko bread crumbs
1½ tsp (9 g) kosher salt
¼ cup (30 g) cream cheese, cut into ¼-inch (6-mm) cubes
1 tbsp (15 ml) avocado or olive oil
1 (10-oz [283-g]) jar pepper jelly

In a mixing bowl combine the beef, eggs, panko and salt. Be careful not to overmix. Scoop a golf ball–sized amount of meat mixture into your hand. Form a ball and press your finger into the middle to form an indent. Place a cube of cream cheese into the indent. Press the meat mixture on top of the cream cheese to form a meatball and to seal the cheese inside. Make sure the filling is completely enclosed. Repeat with the remaining meat mixture and cream cheese to form 28 meatballs total.

Turn the Instant Pot on to sauté mode and add the oil. Sauté the meatballs for about 5 minutes on all sides to brown. Be careful not to overcrowd the pan, you will need to do this in multiple batches. Remove the meatballs and place them in an oven-safe baking dish. I like to use an 8-inch (20-cm) cake pan.

Place 1½ cups (360 ml) of water in the bottom of your Instant Pot insert, no need to clean it, and add the trivet. Place the cake pan on the trivet and close the lid. Make sure the valve is turned to sealing. Cook on steam mode for 6 minutes. Manually release the pressure by carefully moving the valve to venting. Carefully remove the meatballs and toss them with the pepper jelly.

CHEESEBURGER MEATBALLS

2 lbs (907 g) 80/20 ground beef
2 eggs
¼ cup (14 g) panko bread crumbs
1½ tsp (9 g) kosher salt
7 sliced pickle rounds, cut into quarters
2 oz (57 g) cheddar cheese, cut into ¼-inch (6-mm) cubes
1 tbsp (15 ml) avocado or olive oil
Thousand Island dressing, for topping

In a mixing bowl combine the beef, eggs, panko and salt. Be careful not to overmix. Scoop a golf ball–sized amount of meat mixture into your hand. Form a ball and press your finger into the middle to form an indent. Place a quartered pickle and one cube of cheddar cheese into the indent. Press the meat mixture on top of the filling to form a meatball and to seal the cheese and pickle inside. Make sure the filling is completely enclosed. Repeat with the remaining meat mixture, cheddar cheese and pickles to form 28 meatballs total.

Turn the Instant Pot on to sauté mode and add the oil. Sauté the meatballs for about 5 minutes on all sides to brown. Be careful not to overcrowd the pan, you will need to do this in multiple batches. Remove the meatballs and place them in an oven-safe baking dish. I like to use an 8-inch (20-cm) cake pan.

Place 1½ cups (360 ml) of water in the bottom of your Instant Pot insert, no need to clean it, and add the trivet. Place the cake pan on the trivet and close the lid. Make sure the valve is turned to sealing. Cook on steam mode for 6 minutes. Manually release the pressure by carefully moving the valve to venting. Carefully remove the meatballs and place them in your serving dish. Drizzle with Thousand Island dressing.

CHICKEN SALAD

YIELD: 4 SERVINGS

I love that this chicken salad is healthier than a typical recipe. I like to use Greek yogurt to lighten it up. My favorite variation is the Curry Chicken Salad (page 164), which goes perfectly in mini phyllo cups as an easy appetizer. These variations can be served in mini croissants, on crackers, in endives or wrapped in a lavash or tortilla wrap.

CURRY

CLASSIC

THAI

CRANBERRY

CLASSIC CHICKEN SALAD

1 lb (454 g) boneless, skinless chicken breasts
1 cup (240 ml) Greek yogurt
2 tbsp (30 ml) mayonnaise
1 cup (125 g) green apple, diced
¼ cup (25 g) dried cranberries
1 tsp kosher salt
⅛ tsp black pepper
4 croissants, for serving

Add 1 cup (240 ml) of water in the bottom of your Instant Pot insert and add the trivet. Place the chicken on the trivet and close the lid. Make sure the valve is turned to the sealing position. Cook on manual, high pressure for 20 minutes. Naturally release the pressure for 10 minutes then move the valve to venting. Let the chicken cool slightly then cut it into cubes.

Combine the chicken with the yogurt, mayonnaise, apple, cranberries, salt and black pepper until well incorporated. Serve in croissants.

CURRY CHICKEN SALAD

1 lb (454 g) boneless, skinless chicken breasts
1 cup (240 ml) Greek yogurt
2 tbsp (30 ml) mayonnaise
1 cup (125 g) green apple, diced
¼ cup (36 g) golden raisins
1½ tsp (3 g) curry powder
1 tsp kosher salt
4 croissants, for serving

Add 1 cup (240 ml) of water in the bottom of your Instant Pot insert and add the trivet. Place the chicken on the trivet and close the lid. Make sure the valve is turned to the sealing position. Cook on manual, high pressure for 20 minutes. Naturally release the pressure for 10 minutes then move the valve to venting. Let the chicken cool slightly then cut it into cubes.

Combine the chicken with the yogurt, mayonnaise, apple, raisins, curry powder and salt until well incorporated. Serve in croissants.

THAI CHICKEN SALAD

1 lb (454 g) boneless, skinless chicken breasts
1 cup (240 ml) Greek yogurt
2 tbsp (30 ml) mayonnaise
1–2 tbsp (15–30 ml) peanut satay sauce
1 tsp kosher salt
1 tsp cilantro, roughly chopped
1 tsp mint, roughly chopped
4 croissants, for serving
¼ cup (32 g) carrot, julienned, for serving
¼ cup (26 g) cucumber, julienned, for serving

Add 1 cup (240 ml) of water in the bottom of your Instant Pot insert and add the trivet. Place the chicken on the trivet and close the lid. Make sure the valve is turned to the sealing position. Cook on manual, high pressure for 20 minutes. Naturally release the pressure for 10 minutes then move the valve to venting. Let the chicken cool slightly then cut it into cubes.

Combine the chicken with the yogurt, mayonnaise, peanut sauce, salt, cilantro and mint until well incorporated. Serve in croissants with the carrot and cucumber.

See image on page 162.

CRANBERRY CHICKEN SALAD

1 lb (454 g) boneless, skinless chicken breasts
1 cup (240 ml) Greek yogurt
2 tbsp (30 ml) mayonnaise
1 cup (125 g) green apple, diced
¼ cup (60 ml) cranberry sauce
1 tsp kosher salt
⅛ tsp black pepper
4 croissants, for serving

Add 1 cup (240 ml) of water in the bottom of your Instant Pot insert and add the trivet. Place the chicken on the trivet and close the lid. Make sure the valve is turned to the sealing position. Cook on manual, high pressure for 20 minutes. Naturally release the pressure for 10 minutes then move the valve to venting. Let the chicken cool slightly then cut it into cubes.

Combine the chicken with the yogurt, mayonnaise, apple, cranberry sauce, salt and pepper until well incorporated. Serve in croissants.

DEVILED EGGS

YIELD: 24 SERVINGS

Wow your guests with these deviled egg flavor combinations. These recipes use my go-to hard-boiled egg method, and they come out perfectly every time. I have had better luck peeling hard-boiled eggs with white shells as opposed to brown.

CLASSIC

JALAPEÑO-BACON

LOX

CARBONARA

CLASSIC DEVILED EGGS

12 eggs

FOR THE CLASSIC MIX-IN

¼ cup (60 ml) mayonnaise

2 tsp (10 ml) yellow or Dijon mustard

2 tbsp (30 ml) pickle relish

2 tbsp (6 g) chives, finely chopped, divided

¼ tsp kosher salt

⅛ tsp black pepper

3 slices (about 3 tbsp [45 g]) applewood smoked bacon, cooked until crispy and finely chopped, divided

Paprika, for garnish

Place 1 cup (240 ml) of water and the trivet into the Instant Pot insert. Place the eggs on the trivet and close the lid. Make sure the valve is turned to sealing. Cook on manual, high pressure for 7 minutes. Manually release the pressure by carefully moving the valve to venting. Place the eggs in ice water to stop the cooking process.

Peel the eggs and slice them in half. Remove the yolks and press them through a sieve into a medium bowl. Add the mayonnaise, mustard, relish, 1 tablespoon (3 g) of the chives, salt, pepper and 2 tablespoons (30 g) of the bacon and mix to combine. Place the mixture in a plastic storage bag and remove the air. Cut the corner off the bag and pipe the filling into the egg white. Top with the paprika and the remaining bacon and chives.

JALAPEÑO-BACON DEVILED EGGS

12 eggs

FOR THE JALAPEÑO-BACON MIX-IN

4 slices applewood smoked bacon

¼ cup (55 g) brown sugar

2 tbsp (16 g) pickled jalapeño, finely chopped, divided

¼ cup (60 ml) mayonnaise

2 tsp (10 ml) yellow or Dijon mustard

2 tbsp (30 ml) pickle relish

1 tbsp (3 g) chives, finely chopped

¼ tsp kosher salt

⅛ tsp black pepper

Place 1 cup (240 ml) of water and the trivet into the Instant Pot insert. Place the eggs on the trivet and close the lid. Make sure the valve is turned to sealing. Cook on manual, high pressure for 7 minutes. Manually release the pressure by carefully moving the valve to venting. Place the eggs in ice water to stop the cooking process.

Preheat the oven to 400°F (204°C). Place the bacon on a foil-lined baking sheet. Combine the brown sugar with 1 tablespoon (8 g) of the pickled jalapeño and stir until a paste forms. Brush the paste on the bacon and cook in the oven for 15 minutes. Remove and let cool. Roughly chop the bacon.

Peel the eggs and slice them in half. Remove the yolks and press them through a sieve into a medium bowl. Add the remaining tablespoon (8 g) of pickled jalapeño, mayonnaise, mustard, relish, chives, salt and pepper and mix to combine. Place the mixture in a plastic storage bag and remove the air. Cut the corner off the bag and pipe the filling into the egg white. Top with the candied bacon.

See image on page 166.

LOX DEVILED EGGS

12 eggs

FOR THE LOX MIX-IN

¼ cup (60 ml) mayonnaise
1 tbsp (15 g) cream cheese, at room temperature
2 tsp (10 ml) yellow or Dijon mustard
2 tbsp (30 ml) pickle relish
2 tbsp (6 g) chives, finely chopped, divided
¼ tsp kosher salt
⅛ tsp black pepper
3 tbsp (24 g) lox, finely chopped, divided
1 tbsp (10 g) red onion, finely diced
1 tbsp (7 g) capers
Everything bagel seasoning, for garnish

Place 1 cup (240 ml) of water and the trivet into the Instant Pot insert. Place the eggs on the trivet and close the lid. Make sure the valve is turned to sealing. Cook on manual, high pressure for 7 minutes. Manually release the pressure by carefully moving the valve to venting. Place the eggs in ice water to stop the cooking process.

Peel the eggs and slice them in half. Remove the yolks and press them through a sieve into a medium bowl. Add the mayonnaise, cream cheese, mustard, relish, 1 tablespoon (3 g) of the chives, salt, pepper and 2 tablespoons (16 g) of the lox and mix to combine. Place the mixture in a plastic storage bag and remove the air. Cut the corner off the bag and pipe the filling into the egg white. Top with the remaining lox, chives, red onion and capers and sprinkle with the everything bagel seasoning.

CARBONARA DEVILED EGGS

12 eggs

FOR THE CARBONARA MIX-IN

¼ cup (60 ml) mayonnaise
2 tsp (10 ml) yellow or Dijon mustard
2 tbsp (30 ml) pickle relish
1 tbsp (3 g) chives, finely chopped
¼ tsp kosher salt
⅛ tsp black pepper
2 oz (57 g) pancetta, cooked until crispy and finely chopped, divided
Store-bought Parmesan crisps, for garnish
Freshly ground black pepper, to taste

Place 1 cup (240 ml) of water and the trivet into the Instant Pot insert. Place the eggs on the trivet and close the lid. Make sure the valve is turned to sealing. Cook on manual, high pressure for 7 minutes. Manually release the pressure by carefully moving the valve to venting. Place the eggs in ice water to stop the cooking process.

Peel the eggs and slice them in half. Remove the yolks and press them through a sieve into a medium bowl. Add the mayonnaise, mustard, relish, chives, salt, pepper and 1 ounce (29 g) of the pancetta and mix to combine. Place the mixture in a plastic storage bag and remove the air. Cut the corner off the bag and pipe the filling into the egg white. Top with the remaining pancetta, Parmesan crisps and freshly ground black pepper.

CHICKEN WINGS

YIELD: 4 SERVINGS

Chicken wings are always a crowd favorite and these variations
are something your guests will be talking about for a very long time!
You can keep them in the Instant Pot to stay warm for your guests.

PINEAPPLE BBQ

THAI

**BROWN SUGAR–PICKLED
JALAPEÑO**

BUFFALO-RANCH

PINEAPPLE BBQ CHICKEN WINGS

2½ lbs (1.1 kg) chicken wings

FOR THE PINEAPPLE BBQ SAUCE

1 cup (240 ml) ketchup
½ cup (120 ml) pineapple juice
½ tsp garlic powder
½ tsp chili powder

Place 1 cup (240 ml) of water into the Instant Pot insert. Place the chicken in a steamer basket and place it inside the pot. Seal the lid and turn the valve to the sealing position. Cook on manual, high pressure for 15 minutes. Release the pressure manually by carefully moving the valve to venting.

Remove the wings. Combine the ketchup, pineapple juice and garlic and chili powders in a small bowl. Place the wings on a foil-lined baking sheet and brush them with the BBQ sauce on both sides. Broil the wings for 5 minutes. Flip them and broil for another 5 minutes. Brush with any leftover sauce.

See image on page 170.

BROWN SUGAR-PICKLED JALAPEÑO CHICKEN WINGS

2½ lbs (1.1 kg) chicken wings

FOR THE BROWN SUGAR-JALAPEÑO COATING

½ cup (68 g) pickled jalapeños, drained, finely minced
1 cup (220 g) brown sugar
¼ tsp red pepper flakes

Place 1 cup (240 ml) of water into the Instant Pot insert. Place the chicken in a steamer basket and place it inside the pot. Seal the lid and turn the valve to the sealing position. Cook on manual, high pressure for 15 minutes. Release the pressure manually by carefully moving the valve to venting.

Remove the wings. Combine the jalapeños, brown sugar and red pepper flakes in a small bowl. Place the wings on a foil-lined baking sheet and brush them with the coating on both sides. Broil the wings for 5 minutes. Flip them and broil for another 5 minutes. Brush with any leftover sauce.

THAI CHICKEN WINGS

2½ lbs (1.1 kg) chicken wings

FOR THE THAI SAUCE

¼ cup (60 ml) fish sauce

¼ cup (55 g) brown sugar

1 tsp sesame oil

1 tsp lime zest

2 tsp (4 g) ginger, minced

2 tsp (6 g) garlic, minced

1 tsp jalapeño, minced

Place 1 cup (240 ml) of water into the Instant Pot insert. Place the chicken in a steamer basket and place it inside the pot. Seal the lid and turn the valve to the sealing position. Cook on manual, high pressure for 15 minutes. Release the pressure manually by carefully moving the valve to venting.

Remove the wings. Combine the fish sauce, brown sugar, sesame oil, lime zest, ginger, garlic and jalapeño in a small bowl. Place the wings on a foil-lined baking sheet and brush them with the sauce on both sides. Broil the wings for 5 minutes. Flip them and broil for another 5 minutes. Brush with any leftover sauce.

BUFFALO-RANCH CHICKEN WINGS

2½ lbs (1.1 kg) chicken wings

FOR THE BUFFALO-RANCH SAUCE

1 cup (240 ml) buffalo sauce

1 (1-oz [28-g]) packet dry ranch dip mix

Place 1 cup (240 ml) of water into the Instant Pot insert. Place the chicken in a steamer basket and place it inside the pot. Seal the lid and turn the valve to the sealing position. Cook on manual, high pressure for 15 minutes. Release the pressure manually by carefully moving the valve to venting.

Remove the wings. Combine the buffalo sauce and ranch mix in a small bowl. Place the wings on a foil-lined baking sheet and brush them with the sauce on both sides. Broil the wings for 5 minutes. Flip them and broil for another 5 minutes. Brush with any leftover sauce.

SPINACH-ARTICHOKE DIP

YIELD: 8 SERVINGS

This warm, creamy, garlicky dip is delicious with bread, vegetables or chips.
You won't actually be using the pressure button for this recipe, but it's perfect
to make in the Instant Pot for any party since you can keep it warm
with the "keep warm" function.

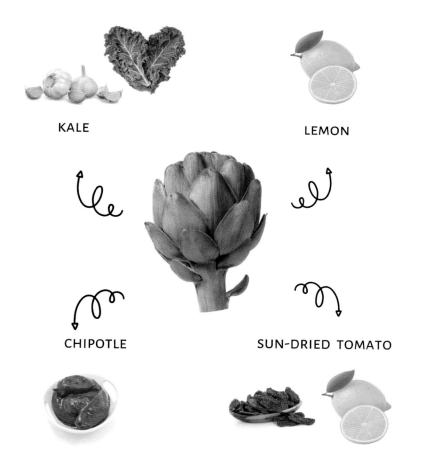

KALE

LEMON

CHIPOTLE

SUN-DRIED TOMATO

KALE SPINACH-ARTICHOKE DIP

1 lb (454 g) cream cheese, diced into 1-inch (3-cm) chunks

2 (14-oz [396-g]) cans artichoke hearts, drained and roughly chopped

1 cup (156 g) frozen spinach, thawed and squeezed dry

2 cups (134 g) kale, finely chopped

4 cloves garlic, finely minced

3 cups (336 g) Italian five cheese blend

1 tsp kosher salt

¼ tsp black pepper

1 loaf sourdough bread, sliced, for serving (optional)

Vegetables of choice, for serving (optional)

Chips, for serving (optional)

Crackers or gluten-free crackers, for serving (optional)

Turn the Instant Pot on to sauté mode. Add all of the ingredients to the pot and stir until the cream cheese is completely melted and well combined. Serve the dip straight from the pot with your choice of sides.

LEMON SPINACH-ARTICHOKE DIP

1 lb (454 g) cream cheese, diced into 1-inch (3-cm) chunks

2 (14-oz [396-g]) cans artichoke hearts, drained and roughly chopped

2 cups (312 g) frozen spinach, thawed and squeezed dry

4 cloves garlic, finely minced

3 cups (336 g) Italian five cheese blend

2 tsp (4 g) lemon zest

1 tsp kosher salt

¼ tsp black pepper

1 loaf sourdough bread, sliced, for serving (optional)

Vegetables of choice, for serving (optional)

Chips, for serving (optional)

Crackers or gluten-free crackers, for serving (optional)

Turn the Instant Pot on to sauté mode. Add all of the ingredients to the pot and stir until the cream cheese is completely melted and well combined. Serve the dip straight from the pot with your choice of sides.

CHIPOTLE SPINACH-ARTICHOKE DIP

1 lb (454 g) cream cheese, diced into 1-inch (3-cm) chunks

2 (14-oz [396-g]) cans artichoke hearts, drained and roughly chopped

2 cups (312 g) frozen spinach, thawed and squeezed dry

4 cloves garlic, finely minced

3 cups (336 g) Italian five cheese blend

2 tsp (6 g) chipotle in adobo

1 tsp kosher salt

¼ tsp black pepper

1 loaf sourdough bread, sliced, for serving (optional)

Vegetables of choice, for serving (optional)

Chips, for serving (optional)

Crackers or gluten-free crackers, for serving (optional)

Turn the Instant Pot on to sauté mode. Add all of the ingredients to the pot and stir until the cream cheese is completely melted and well combined. Serve the dip straight from the pot with your choice of sides.

SUN-DRIED TOMATO SPINACH-ARTICHOKE DIP

1 lb (454 g) cream cheese, diced into 1-inch (3-cm) chunks

2 (14-oz [396-g]) cans artichoke hearts, drained and roughly chopped

2 cups (312 g) frozen spinach, thawed and squeezed dry

¼ cup (14 g) sun-dried tomatoes, roughly chopped

4 cloves garlic, finely minced

3 cups (336 g) Italian five cheese blend

1 tsp kosher salt

¼ tsp black pepper

1 loaf sourdough bread, sliced, for serving (optional)

Vegetables of choice, for serving (optional)

Chips, for serving (optional)

Crackers or gluten-free crackers, for serving (optional)

Turn the Instant Pot on to sauté mode. Add all of the ingredients to the pot and stir until the cream cheese is completely melted and well combined. Serve the dip straight from the pot with your choice of sides.

*See image on page 174.

BRAZILIAN BITES

YIELD: 21 BITES

Brazilian cheese bread, *pao de queijo*, is a roll made out of tapioca flour and typically has a crunchy outer shell with a soft, chewy middle. I started making them in the Instant Pot, and they come out great! These little bites are perfect for a bite-sized appetizer, and you can flavor them however you like. My favorite are the Lemon-Rosemary Brazilian Bites (page 181). You can also serve these as a side dish!

TACO

PARMESAN

LEMON-ROSEMARY

PIZZA

PARMESAN BRAZILIAN BITES

1 cup (240 ml) whole milk
½ cup (60 ml) vegetable oil
1 tsp kosher salt
2 cups (250 g) tapioca flour
2 eggs
2 cups (200 g) Parmesan cheese, shredded

Place the milk, oil and salt in a saucepan heated over medium heat. Bring the mixture to a simmer. Once the liquid has simmered, place it in a stand mixer fitted with a dough hook and add the flour. Mix at medium speed. Add the eggs, one at a time, until each egg is completely incorporated. Add the Parmesan and stir to combine. Place a spoonful of batter into a silicone mold filling it three-fourths of the way up. Cover the mold with a paper towel and then with foil.

Add 1 cup (240 ml) of water into the insert and add the trivet. Place the mold on top of the trivet and seal with the lid. Turn the valve to sealing and cook on manual, high pressure for 20 minutes. Manually release the pressure by carefully moving the valve to venting. Remove the bites from the mold and place them on a foil-lined baking sheet. Place the bites under the broiler for 3 to 5 minutes, or until golden brown, checking halfway through and rotating the pan.

PIZZA BRAZILIAN BITES

1 cup (240 ml) whole milk
½ cup (60 ml) vegetable oil
1 tsp kosher salt
2 cups (250 g) tapioca flour
2 eggs
2 cups (200 g) Parmesan cheese, shredded
½ cup (60 g) sliced pepperoni, diced small

Place the milk, oil and salt in a saucepan heated over medium heat. Bring the mixture to a simmer. Once the liquid has simmered, place it in a stand mixer fitted with a dough hook and add the flour. Mix at medium speed. Add the eggs, one at a time, until each egg is completely incorporated. Add the Parmesan and pepperoni and stir to combine. Place a spoonful of batter into a silicone mold filling it three-fourths of the way up. Cover the mold with a paper towel and then with foil.

Add 1 cup (240 ml) of water into the insert and add the trivet. Place the mold on top of the trivet and seal with the lid. Turn the valve to sealing and cook on manual, high pressure for 20 minutes. Manually release the pressure by carefully moving the valve to venting. Remove the bites from the mold and place them on a foil-lined baking sheet. Place the bites under the broiler for 3 to 5 minutes, or until golden brown, checking halfway through and rotating the pan.

*See image on page 178.

LEMON-ROSEMARY BRAZILIAN BITES

1 cup (240 ml) whole milk

½ cup (60 ml) vegetable oil

1 tsp kosher salt

2 cups (250 g) tapioca flour

2 eggs

2 cups (200 g) Parmesan cheese, shredded

1 tbsp (2 g) rosemary, minced

1 tsp lemon zest

Place the milk, oil and salt in a saucepan heated over medium heat. Bring the mixture to a simmer. Once the liquid has simmered, place it in a stand mixer fitted with a dough hook and add the flour. Mix at medium speed. Add the eggs, one at a time, until each egg is completely incorporated. Add the Parmesan, rosemary and lemon zest and stir to combine. Place a spoonful of batter into a silicone mold filling it three-fourths of the way up. Cover the mold with a paper towel and then with foil.

Add 1 cup (240 ml) of water into the insert and add the trivet. Place the mold on top of the trivet and seal with the lid. Turn the valve to sealing and cook on manual, high pressure for 20 minutes. Manually release the pressure by carefully moving the valve to venting. Remove the bread bites from the mold and place them on a foil-lined baking sheet. Place the bites under the broiler for 3 to 5 minutes, or until golden brown, checking halfway through and rotating the pan.

TACO BRAZILIAN BITES

1 cup (240 ml) whole milk

½ cup (60 ml) vegetable oil

1 tsp kosher salt

2 cups (250 g) tapioca flour

2 eggs

2 cups (200 g) Parmesan cheese, shredded

2 tsp (7 g) taco seasoning

Place the milk, oil and salt in a saucepan heated over medium heat. Bring the mixture to a simmer. Once the liquid has simmered, place it in a stand mixer fitted with a dough hook and add the flour. Mix at medium speed. Add the eggs, one at a time, until each egg is completely incorporated. Add the Parmesan and taco seasoning and stir to combine. Place a spoonful of batter into a silicone mold filling it three-fourths of the way up. Cover the mold with a paper towel and then with foil.

Add 1 cup (240 ml) of water into the insert and add the trivet. Place the mold on top of the trivet and seal with the lid. Turn the valve to sealing and cook on manual, high pressure for 20 minutes. Manually release the pressure by carefully moving the valve to venting. Remove the bread bites from the mold and place them on a foil-lined baking sheet. Place the bites under the broiler for 3 to 5 minutes, or until golden brown, checking halfway through and rotating the pan.

HUMMUS

YIELD: 6 CUPS (1.5 KG)

Hummus in the Instant Pot is quick and easy. I especially love Everything but the Bagel Hummus (page 185). It is delicious when served with a variety of vegetables, crackers, pita chips, or even as a delicious spread on a vegetarian sandwich. I also make a big batch of hummus and store it in an airtight container for a healthy snack to have throughout the week.

EVERYTHING BUT THE BAGEL

CHIPOTLE

JALAPEÑO-CILANTRO

HARISSA

HARISSA HUMMUS

1 lb (454 g) dried garbanzo beans
¼ cup plus 1 tbsp (75 ml) tahini
2 tsp (12 g) kosher salt, or to taste
¼ cup (60 ml) lemon juice
Zest of 2 lemons
2 tsp (10 g) harissa

Soak the beans in 4 cups (960 ml) of water for at least 6 hours or overnight. Drain and rinse with cold water. Add the beans to the Instant Pot with 4 cups (960 ml) of water and make sure the valve is turned to the sealing position. Cook on manual, high pressure for 15 minutes. Naturally release the pressure for 15 minutes, then move the valve to venting.

Remove 2 cups (480 ml) of the cooking liquid and set aside. Drain the beans. Place the beans in a food processor and add the tahini, salt, lemon juice and zest and harissa. Pulse to blend. Slowly add the reserved cooking liquid to thin the hummus to your desired thickness and consistency.

JALAPEÑO-CILANTRO HUMMUS

1 lb (454 g) dried garbanzo beans
¼ cup plus 1 tbsp (75 ml) tahini
2 tsp (12 g) kosher salt, or to taste
¼ cup (60 ml) lemon juice
Zest of 2 lemons
½ small jalapeño, seeds removed and minced, or to taste
¼ cup (4 g) cilantro

Soak the beans in 4 cups (960 ml) of water for at least 6 hours or overnight. Drain and rinse with cold water. Add the beans to the Instant Pot with 4 cups (960 ml) of water and make sure the valve is turned to the sealing position. Cook on manual, high pressure for 15 minutes. Naturally release the pressure for 15 minutes, then move the valve to venting.

Remove 2 cups (480 ml) of the cooking liquid and set aside. Drain the beans. Place the beans in a food processor and add the tahini, salt, lemon juice and zest, jalapeño and cilantro. Pulse to blend. Slowly add the reserved cooking liquid to thin the hummus out to your desired thickness and consistency.

EVERYTHING BUT THE BAGEL HUMMUS

1 lb (454 g) dried garbanzo beans
¼ cup plus 1 tbsp (75 ml) tahini
2 tsp (12 g) kosher salt, or to taste
¼ cup (60 ml) lemon juice
Zest of 2 lemons
1 tbsp (10 g) everything bagel seasoning

Soak the beans in 4 cups (960 ml) of water for at least 6 hours or overnight. Drain and rinse with cold water. Add the beans to the Instant Pot with 4 cups (960 ml) of water and make sure the valve is turned to the sealing position. Cook on manual, high pressure for 15 minutes. Naturally release the pressure for 15 minutes, then move the valve to venting.

Remove 2 cups (480 ml) of the cooking liquid and set aside. Drain the beans. Place the beans in a food processor and add the tahini, salt, lemon juice and zest and everything bagel seasoning. Pulse to blend. Slowly add the reserved cooking liquid to thin the hummus out to your desired thickness and consistency.

CHIPOTLE HUMMUS

1 lb (454 g) dried garbanzo beans
¼ cup plus 1 tbsp (75 ml) tahini
2 tsp (12 g) kosher salt, or to taste
¼ cup (60 ml) lemon juice
Zest of 2 lemons
2 tbsp (34 g) chipotle in adobo

Soak the beans in 4 cups (960 ml) of water for at least 6 hours or overnight. Drain and rinse with cold water. Add the beans to the Instant Pot with 4 cups (960 ml) of water and make sure the valve is turned to the sealing position. Cook on manual, high pressure for 15 minutes. Naturally release the pressure for 15 minutes, then move the valve to venting.

Remove 2 cups (480 ml) of the cooking liquid and set aside. Drain the beans. Place the beans in a food processor and add the tahini, salt, lemon juice and zest and chipotle. Pulse to blend. Slowly add the reserved cooking liquid to thin the hummus out to your desired thickness and consistency.

*See image on page 182.

SIDES

If you are anything like me, you love your sides! I love having healthy sides to serve with dinner, and I love it even more when I make extra to have on hand for lunches the next day. I especially love making the Tabbouleh Quinoa (page 190) or Fried Rice (page 194). These make meal prep easy, and I get lunch done for the whole week!

These Instant Pot sides are some of my absolute favorites. I love how the Instant Pot cooks so consistently so you know your sides won't be overcooked. No more mushy green beans here!

QUINOA

YIELD: 6 SERVINGS

Fluffy quinoa mixed with some delicious mix-ins! What could be better than that? I love making a big batch of quinoa to serve as a side for dinner and then morphing it into an easy lunch the next day. It is also great to meal prep for the whole week.

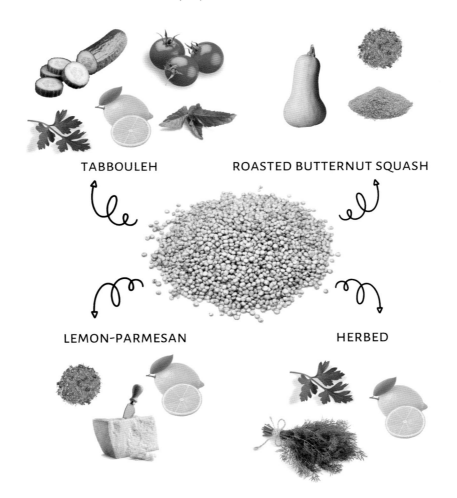

TABBOULEH

ROASTED BUTTERNUT SQUASH

LEMON-PARMESAN

HERBED

TABBOULEH QUINOA

2 cups (340 g) quinoa, rinsed with cold water
2½ cups (600 ml) chicken stock
¼ cup (40 g) red onion, finely diced
½ cup (52 g) cucumber, diced
¾ cup (135 g) tomatoes, diced
2 tbsp (11 g) mint, roughly chopped
¼ cup (15 g) flat leaf parsley, roughly chopped
Zest of 2 lemons
¼ cup (60 ml) lemon juice
¼ cup (60 ml) olive oil
1 tsp kosher salt
¼ tsp black pepper

Place the quinoa and stock into the Instant Pot insert. Seal the lid and move the valve to the sealing position. Cook on manual, high pressure for 1 minute. Let the pressure release naturally until the red pin drops. Remove the lid and fluff the quinoa with a fork. Let cool for 5 minutes and then combine the quinoa with the rest of the ingredients. This dish can be served cold or at room temperature.

See image on page 188.

ROASTED BUTTERNUT SQUASH QUINOA

2 tbsp (28 g) unsalted butter
1 lb (454 g) butternut squash, peeled, seeds removed and diced
1½ tsp (2 g) Italian seasoning, divided
2 tbsp (28 g) brown sugar, divided
1½ tsp (9 g) kosher salt, divided
2 cups (340 g) quinoa, rinsed with cold water
2½ cups (600 ml) chicken stock

Turn the Instant Pot on to sauté mode. Add the butter, squash, ½ teaspoon of Italian seasoning, 1 tablespoon (14 g) of brown sugar and ½ teaspoon of salt and cook for 15 minutes, stirring occasionally. Remove the squash and set aside. Clean the insert. Place the quinoa and stock into the Instant Pot insert. Seal the lid and move the valve to the sealing position. Cook on manual, high pressure for 1 minute. Let the pressure release naturally until the red pin drops. Remove the lid and fluff the quinoa with a fork. Let the quinoa cool for 5 minutes and then combine it with the squash, remaining Italian seasoning, brown sugar and salt. It can be served cold or at room temperature.

LEMON-PARMESAN QUINOA

2 cups (340 g) quinoa, rinsed with cold water
2½ cups (600 ml) chicken stock
1 tsp kosher salt
1 tsp Italian seasoning
¼ cup (25 g) Parmesan cheese, shredded
Zest of 1 lemon

Place the quinoa and stock into the Instant Pot insert. Seal the lid and move the valve to the sealing position. Cook on manual, high pressure for 1 minute. Let the pressure release naturally until the red pin drops. Remove the lid and fluff the quinoa with a fork. Let cool for 5 minutes and then combine the quinoa with the salt, Italian seasoning, Parmesan and lemon zest. This dish can be served cold or at room temperature.

HERBED QUINOA

2 cups (340 g) quinoa, rinsed with cold water
2½ cups (600 ml) chicken stock
1 tsp kosher salt
2 tsp (2 g) dill, roughly chopped
2 tsp (2 g) flat leaf parsley, roughly chopped
Juice of 1 lemon

Place the quinoa and stock into the Instant Pot insert. Seal the lid and move the valve to the sealing position. Cook on manual, high pressure for 1 minute. Let the pressure release naturally until the red pin drops. Remove the lid and fluff the quinoa with a fork. Let cool for 5 minutes and then combine the quinoa with the salt, dill, parsley and lemon juice. This dish can be served cold or room temperature.

RICE

YIELD: 6 SERVINGS

Rice is one of the first things I ever made in my Instant Pot. It is important to wash your rice under cold water to remove any extra starch. Excess starch can cause your rice to become sticky and gummy. Make sure you try out the Fried Rice (page 194). It's a go-to meal prep item for my family. I double the batch and have leftovers for lunch the whole week.

FRIED

COCONUT

MEXICAN

YOGURT

FRIED RICE

1 tbsp (15 ml) sesame oil
2 cups (300 g) ham, cubed
2 cups (400 g) white rice, rinsed
2 cups (480 ml) water
1 cup (330 g) fresh or canned pineapple, cubed
4 tbsp (57 g) unsalted butter
1 cup (124 g) frozen mixed vegetables
2½ tbsp (37 ml) liquid aminos, such as Bragg Liquid Aminos
½ tsp kosher salt
¼ tsp black pepper

Turn the Instant Pot on to sauté mode. Add the sesame oil and ham and cook for 5 to 7 minutes to caramelize the ham. Remove the ham and set aside. Clean the insert. Add the rice and water. Seal the lid and turn the valve to the sealing position. Turn the Instant Pot on manual, high pressure for 10 minutes. Let the pressure release naturally for 10 minutes. Fluff the rice with a fork and add the pineapple, butter, vegetables, liquid aminos, salt and pepper. Mix together with a fork to prevent the rice from becoming too sticky.

*See image on page 192.

MEXICAN RICE

2 cups (400 g) white rice, rinsed
2 cups (480 ml) water
1 (12-oz [340-g]) jar red salsa

Place the rice, water and salsa into the Instant Pot insert. Seal the lid and turn the valve to the sealing position. Turn the Instant Pot on manual, high pressure for 10 minutes. Let the pressure release naturally for 10 minutes. Fluff the rice with a fork before serving.

COCONUT RICE

2 cups (400 g) white rice, rinsed
1 (13.5-oz [382-g]) can coconut milk
¼ cup (60 ml) water
1 tsp kosher salt
1 tbsp (15 g) granulated sugar

Place all of the ingredients into the Instant Pot insert. Seal the lid and turn the valve to the sealing position. Turn the Instant Pot on manual, high pressure for 10 minutes. Let the pressure release naturally for 10 minutes. Fluff the rice with a fork before serving.

YOGURT RICE SALAD

2 cups (400 g) white rice, rinsed
2 cups (480 ml) water
¼ cup (57 g) unsalted butter
1 tsp dry mustard seeds
½ tsp curry powder
1 cup (240 ml) plain Greek yogurt
1 tsp kosher salt
2 tsp (1 g) cilantro, roughly chopped
2 tsp (2 g) green onion, chopped

Place the rice and water into the Instant Pot insert. Seal the lid and turn the valve to the sealing position. Turn the Instant Pot on manual, high pressure for 10 minutes. Let the pressure release naturally for 10 minutes. Heat the butter and mustard seeds in a small skillet over medium heat until the butter is melted. Pour the butter into the rice and fluff with a fork. Add the curry powder, yogurt, salt, cilantro and green onion and stir until combined.

MASHED POTATOES

YIELD: 6 SERVINGS

I love making mashed potatoes in the Instant Pot, especially for a gathering. I keep the mashed potatoes in the pot with the lid on so they stay hot and fresh until I arrive. If the potatoes dry out or become too thick, just add a little extra cream or milk and stir them up right before serving. You can use Russet, yellow or red potatoes for mashed potatoes.

SWEET POTATO–CARROT

BOURSIN

BROWNED BUTTER SAGE

LOADED

BROWNED BUTTER SAGE MASHED POTATOES

½ cup (114 g) unsalted butter

20 sage leaves

6 large potatoes, peeled and cut into 1-inch (3-cm) chunks (about 10 cups [1.5 kg])

2 cups (480 ml) heavy cream

1–2 tsp (6–12 g) kosher salt

¼ tsp black pepper

Turn the Instant Pot on to sauté mode. Place the butter and sage into the insert for 4 minutes to brown the butter. Remove the butter and sage and set aside. Chop the sage into small pieces.

Add 1 cup (240 ml) of water to the bottom of the insert. Fill a steamer basket with the potatoes and place it in the insert. Seal the lid and turn the valve to the sealing position. Turn the Instant Pot on manual, high pressure for 12 minutes. Release the pressure manually by carefully moving the valve to venting. Remove the basket. Remove any excess liquid left in the bottom of the insert. Place the potatoes, butter and sage back into the insert along with the cream, salt and pepper and mash the mixture with a potato masher until it reaches the desired consistency.

BOURSIN MASHED POTATOES

6 large potatoes, peeled and cut into 1-inch (3-cm) chunks (about 10 cups [1.5 kg])

1 (5.2-oz [150-g]) block Boursin cheese

2 cups (480 ml) heavy cream

1 (4-oz [113-g]) stick unsalted butter

½–1 tsp kosher salt

¼ tsp black pepper

Add 1 cup (240 ml) of water to the bottom of the insert. Fill a steamer basket with the potatoes and place it in the insert. Seal the lid and turn the valve to the sealing position. Turn the Instant Pot on manual, high pressure for 12 minutes. Release the pressure manually by carefully moving the valve to venting. Remove the basket. Remove any excess liquid left in the bottom of the insert. Place the potatoes back into the insert along with the Boursin cheese, heavy cream, butter, salt and pepper and mash the mixture with a potato masher until it reaches the desired consistency.

LOADED MASHED POTATOES

6 slices applewood smoked bacon

6 large potatoes, peeled and cut into 1-inch (3-cm) chunks (about 10 cups [1.5 kg])

2 cups (480 ml) heavy cream

1 (4-oz [113-g]) stick unsalted butter

1½ cups (170 g) shredded cheddar cheese

½–1 tsp kosher salt

¼ tsp black pepper

2 tbsp (6 g) chives, minced

2 tbsp (30 ml) sour cream

Turn the Instant Pot on to sauté mode. Place the bacon slices into the insert and cook until crispy, about 10 minutes. Remove any excess grease. Chop the bacon and set aside.

Add 1 cup (240 ml) of water to the bottom of the insert. Fill a steamer basket with the potatoes and place it in the insert. Seal the lid and turn the valve to the sealing position. Turn the Instant Pot on manual, high pressure for 12 minutes. Release the pressure manually by carefully moving the valve to venting. Remove the basket. Remove any excess liquid left in the bottom of the insert. Place the potatoes back into the insert along with the cream, butter, cheddar cheese, salt and pepper and mash the mixture with a potato masher until it reaches the desired consistency. Top the mashed potatoes with the bacon pieces, chives and sour cream.

See image on page 196.

MASHED CARROTS AND SWEET POTATOES

2 large sweet potatoes, peeled and cut into 1-inch (3-cm) chunks (about 4 cups [536 g])

5 large carrots, peeled and cut into 1-inch (3-cm) pieces (about 2 cups [256 g])

4 tbsp (57 g) unsalted butter

½–1 tsp kosher salt

¼ tsp black pepper

Add 1 cup (240 ml) of water to the bottom of the insert. Fill a steamer basket with the sweet potatoes and carrots and place it in the insert. Seal the lid and turn the valve to the sealing position. Turn the Instant Pot on manual, high pressure for 12 minutes. Release the pressure manually by carefully moving the valve to venting. Remove the basket. Remove any excess liquid left in the bottom of the insert. Place the sweet potato and carrot mixture back into the insert along with the butter, salt and pepper and mash the mixture with a potato masher until it reaches the desired consistency.

BEANS

YIELD: 6 SERVINGS

The Instant Pot cooks beans so evenly. I especially love making Refried Beans (page 203) in the Instant Pot because they are so much healthier than the canned options. They come out creamy and full of flavor without a bunch of fat. I make a big batch of these and make bean and cheese burritos to freeze for my kids when they need a quick lunch.

MEXICAN

REFRIED

BBQ BAKED

BLACK

MEXICAN BEANS

2 cups (288 g) dry Anasazi or pinto beans

1 tbsp (14 g) unsalted butter

1 cup (160 g) white or yellow onion, diced

4 cloves garlic, minced

3 cups (720 ml) chicken or beef stock

1 tbsp (21 g) jalapeño, diced

1 bay leaf

1 tsp garlic salt

1 tsp oregano

2 tsp (12 g) kosher salt

Soak the beans in 4 cups (960 ml) of water for at least 6 hours or overnight. Drain the beans once soaked. Turn the Instant Pot on to sauté mode. Add the butter, onion and garlic. Sauté for 3 minutes. Add the stock, jalapeño, bay leaf, garlic salt, oregano, salt and the drained beans. Seal with the lid and turn the valve to sealing. Turn on manual, high pressure for 30 minutes. Manually release the pressure by carefully moving the valve to venting. Remove the bay leaf before serving.

*See image on page 200.

BBQ BAKED BEANS

2 cups (288 g) dry Anasazi or pinto beans

4 slices applewood smoked bacon

1 cup (160 g) white onion, diced

4 cups (960 ml) chicken stock

¾ cup (180 ml) ketchup

1 tsp Dijon mustard

2 tsp (12 g) kosher salt

½ cup (120 ml) BBQ sauce

3 cups (720 ml) water

Soak the beans in 4 cups (960 ml) of water for at least 6 hours or overnight. Drain the beans once soaked. Turn the Instant Pot on to sauté mode. Sauté the bacon until crispy, about 10 minutes. Remove the bacon and dice into small pieces. Add the onion and sauté for 3 minutes. Add the stock, ketchup, mustard, salt, BBQ sauce, water, bacon and drained beans into the pot. Seal with the lid and turn the valve to sealing. Turn on manual, high pressure for 30 minutes. Manually release the pressure by carefully moving the valve to venting.

BLACK BEANS

2 cups (388 g) dry black beans
1 tbsp (14 g) unsalted butter
1 cup (160 g) white or yellow onion, diced
2 cloves garlic, minced
3 cups (720 ml) chicken or beef stock
2 bay leaves
2 tbsp (42 g) jalapeño, diced
1 tsp cumin
1 tsp oregano
1 tsp kosher salt
12 oz (340 g) premade pico de gallo

Soak the beans in 4 cups (960 ml) of water for at least 6 hours or overnight. Drain the beans once soaked. Turn the Instant Pot on to sauté mode. Add the butter, onion and garlic. Sauté for 3 minutes. Add the stock, bay leaves, jalapeño, cumin, oregano, salt and drained beans. Seal with the lid and turn the valve to sealing. Turn on manual, high pressure for 30 minutes. Manually release the pressure by carefully moving the valve to venting. Remove the bay leaves and stir in the pico de gallo before serving.

REFRIED BEANS

2 cups (288 g) dry Anasazi or pinto beans
1 tbsp (14 g) unsalted butter
1 cup (160 g) white or yellow onion, diced
3 cloves garlic, minced
3 cups (720 ml) chicken or beef stock
2 bay leaves
2 tsp (12 g) kosher salt

Soak the beans in 4 cups (960 ml) of water for at least 6 hours or overnight. Drain the beans once soaked. Turn the Instant Pot on to sauté mode. Add the butter, onion and garlic. Sauté for 3 minutes. Add the stock, bay leaves, salt and drained beans. Seal with the lid and turn the valve to sealing. Turn on manual, high pressure for 30 minutes. Manually release the pressure by carefully moving the valve to venting. Remove the bay leaves and blend with an immersion blender until slightly chunky.

POTATO SALAD

YIELD: 5 SERVINGS

I love potato salad with baby Dutch yellow potatoes. They are the tiny little potatoes. If you can't find them, you can also use a red potato for this recipe. Cut them into a medium dice and cook them on manual, high pressure in the steamer basket for 5 minutes. The classic potato salad is my go-to side dish for a family BBQ and it's the perfect blend of creamy textures and tangy flavors.

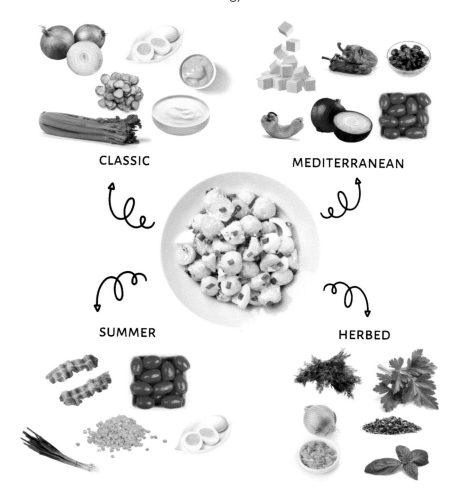

CLASSIC

MEDITERRANEAN

SUMMER

HERBED

CLASSIC POTATO SALAD

1½ lbs (680 g) baby Dutch yellow potatoes, cut in half
½ cup (51 g) celery, diced small
½ cup (71 g) dill pickles, diced small
¼ cup (40 g) white onion, diced small
½ cup (120 ml) mayonnaise
½ cup (120 ml) Greek yogurt
1 tbsp (15 ml) yellow mustard
3 hard-boiled eggs, diced
Kosher salt and pepper, to taste

Add 1 cup (240 ml) of water to the bottom of the insert. Fill a steamer basket with the potatoes and place it in the insert. Seal the lid and turn the valve to the sealing position. Turn the Instant Pot on manual, high pressure for 5 minutes. Release the pressure manually by carefully moving the valve to venting. Remove the basket. Let the potatoes cool to room temperature. Combine the potatoes with the celery, pickles, onion, mayonnaise, yogurt, mustard, eggs, salt and pepper and keep refrigerated until ready to serve.

SUMMER POTATO SALAD

1½ lbs (680 g) baby Dutch yellow potatoes, cut in half
5 slices bacon, cooked until crispy and roughly chopped
1 cup (154 g) corn, roasted
½ cup (75 g) cherry tomatoes, sliced in half
4 hard-boiled eggs, diced
2 tbsp (6 g) chives, minced

FOR THE DRESSING

½ cup (120 ml) mayonnaise
½ cup (120 ml) Greek yogurt
2 tsp (10 ml) whole grain mustard
2 tsp (10 ml) white balsamic vinegar
½ cup (71 g) good quality dill pickles, diced
Kosher salt and black pepper, to taste

Add 1 cup (240 ml) of water to the bottom of the insert. Fill a steamer basket with the potatoes and place it in the insert. Seal the lid and turn the valve to the sealing position. Turn the Instant Pot on manual, high pressure for 5 minutes. Release the pressure manually by carefully moving the valve to venting. Remove the basket. Let the potatoes cool to room temperature. To make the dressing, combine the mayonnaise, yogurt, mustard, vinegar, pickles, salt and pepper and pour it over the potatoes. Add the bacon, corn, tomatoes, eggs and chives and stir to combine. Keep refrigerated until ready to serve.

*See image on page 204.

MEDITERRANEAN POTATO SALAD

1½ lbs (680 g) baby Dutch yellow potatoes, cut in half
½ cup (112 g) jarred roasted bell peppers, sliced
¼ cup (30 g) sliced pepperoncini
½ cup (75 g) cherry tomatoes, sliced in half
2 tbsp (16 g) kalamata olives, pitted and sliced
2 tbsp (20 g) red onion, diced small
2 tbsp (19 g) feta cheese, crumbled
½ cup (120 ml) Italian dressing or to taste

Add 1 cup (240 ml) of water in the bottom of the insert. Fill a steamer basket with the potatoes and place it in the insert. Seal the lid and turn the valve to the sealing position. Turn the Instant Pot on manual, high pressure for 5 minutes. Release the pressure manually by carefully moving the valve to venting. Remove the basket. Let the potatoes cool to room temperature. Combine the potatoes with the peppers, pepperoncini, tomatoes, olives, onion, feta cheese and Italian dressing and keep refrigerated until ready to serve.

HERBED POTATO SALAD

1 tbsp (14 g) unsalted butter
½ cup (57 g) white onion, sliced thinly
1½ lbs (680 g) baby Dutch yellow potatoes, cut in half
5 basil leaves, sliced into chiffonade (see Note on page 44)
1 tbsp (4 g) Italian parsley, roughly chopped
1 tbsp (3 g) dill, roughly chopped
⅛–¼ tsp red pepper flakes, to taste
2 tbsp (30 ml) white balsamic vinegar
2 tbsp (30 ml) extra-virgin olive oil
Kosher salt and black pepper to taste

Turn the Instant Pot on to sauté mode. Add the butter and onion and caramelize for 10 minutes, stirring occasionally. Remove and set aside. Add 1 cup (240 ml) of water to the bottom of the insert. Fill a steamer basket with the potatoes and place it in the insert. Seal the lid and turn the valve to the sealing position. Turn the Instant Pot on manual, high pressure for 5 minutes. Release the pressure manually by carefully moving the valve to venting. Remove the basket. Let the potatoes cool to room temperature. Combine the potatoes with the onion, basil, parsley, dill, red pepper flakes, vinegar, oil, salt and pepper and keep refrigerated until ready to serve.

GREEN BEANS

YIELD: 4-6 SERVINGS

No more soggy green beans! These green beans only need 1 minute in the Instant Pot, and they come out perfectly every time. If you want to make green beans ahead of time, follow the cooking instructions and then submerge the beans into an ice bath before you toss them with the remaining ingredients. This will stop the cooking process and ensure you have vibrant green beans.

LEMON-DILL

BALSAMIC-BACON

SUMMER

CITRUS

LEMON-DILL GREEN BEANS

1 lb (454 g) green beans
1 tbsp (15 ml) olive oil
1 tbsp (3 g) fresh dill, chopped
Zest of 1 lemon
1 tbsp (15 ml) lemon juice
½ tsp kosher salt

Place 1 cup (240 ml) of water along with the trivet into the Instant Pot insert. Fill a steamer basket with the green beans and place it on the trivet. Seal the lid and turn the valve to the sealing position. Turn the Instant Pot on the steam setting for 1 minute. Release the pressure manually by carefully moving the valve to venting. Remove the green beans and toss them with the oil, dill, lemon zest and juice and salt before serving.

See image on page 208.

BALSAMIC-BACON GREEN BEANS

4 slices applewood smoked bacon
1 tbsp (14 g) unsalted butter
1 small yellow onion, sliced thinly
1 lb (454 g) green beans
2 tbsp (30 ml) balsamic vinegar
¼ tsp kosher salt

Turn the Instant Pot on to sauté mode. Cook the bacon until crispy, about 5 minutes. Set aside and roughly chop. Clean out the insert. Add the butter and onion and sauté for 5 minutes then remove and set aside. Place 1 cup (240 ml) of water along with the trivet into the Instant Pot insert. Fill a steamer basket with the green beans and place it on the trivet. Seal the lid and turn the valve to the sealing position. Turn the Instant Pot on the steam setting for 1 minute. Release the pressure manually by carefully moving the valve to venting. Remove the green beans and toss them with the reserved bacon, onion, vinegar and salt.

CITRUS GREEN BEANS

1 lb (454 g) green beans
1 tbsp (14 g) unsalted butter
½ tsp lemon zest
½ tsp orange zest
5 basil leaves, sliced into chiffonade (see Note on page 44)
¼ tsp kosher salt

Place 1 cup (240 ml) of water along with the trivet into the Instant Pot insert. Fill a steamer basket with the green beans and place it on the trivet. Seal the lid and turn the valve to the sealing position. Turn the Instant Pot on the steam setting for 1 minute. Release the pressure manually by carefully moving the valve to venting. Remove the green beans and toss them with the butter, lemon zest, orange zest, basil and salt.

SUMMER GREEN BEANS

4 slices applewood smoked bacon
1 lb (454 g) green beans
1 tbsp (14 g) unsalted butter, melted
½ tsp lemon zest
5 basil leaves, sliced into chiffonade (see Note on page 44)
¼ tsp kosher salt
2 tbsp (19 g) feta cheese, crumbled
¼ cup (37 g) cherry tomatoes, sliced in half
¼ cup (39 g) corn, roasted

Turn the Instant Pot on to sauté mode. Cook the bacon until crispy, about 5 minutes. Set aside and roughly chop. Clean out the insert. Place 1 cup (240 ml) of water along with the trivet into the Instant Pot insert. Fill a steamer basket with the green beans and place it on the trivet. Seal the lid and turn the valve to the sealing position. Turn the Instant Pot on the steam setting for 1 minute. Release the pressure manually by carefully moving the valve to venting. Remove the green beans and toss them with the reserved bacon, butter, lemon zest, basil and salt. Top the beans with the feta cheese, tomatoes and corn.

CORNBREAD

YIELD: 8 SERVINGS

Moist, delicious cornbread is the perfect side for any get-together. I especially love the slightly sweet version of cinnamon and honey.

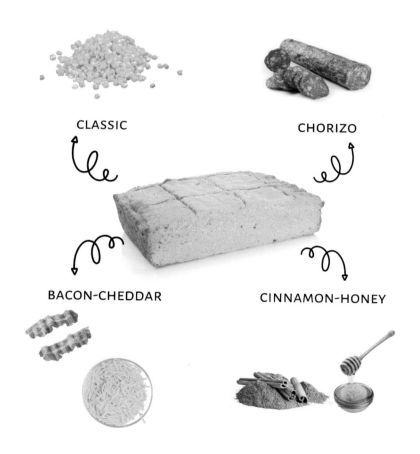

CLASSIC

CHORIZO

BACON-CHEDDAR

CINNAMON-HONEY

CLASSIC CORNBREAD

1 cup (125 g) all-purpose flour

1 cup (122 g) yellow cornmeal

½ tsp kosher salt

1 tbsp plus 1 tsp (18 g) baking powder

1 cup (200 g) granulated sugar

1 (15-oz [425-g]) can creamed corn

1 cup (227 g) unsalted butter, melted, plus more for serving

4 eggs

Spray an 8-inch (20-cm) cake pan, or a pan that will fit inside your insert, with cooking spray. Combine the flour, cornmeal, salt, baking powder and sugar in a mixing bowl. Add the creamed corn, butter and eggs and stir to combine. Add the batter to the prepared pan. Cover with foil. Depending on the size of your Instant Pot, you may have to cook the cornbread in two batches.

Place 1 cup (240 ml) of water in the bottom of the Instant Pot insert, add the trivet and place the cake pan on top of it. Seal the lid and turn the valve to the sealing position. Turn the Instant Pot on manual, high pressure for 45 minutes. Release the pressure manually by carefully moving the valve to venting. Carefully remove the cake pan and remove the foil. Cut the cornbread into 8 slices and serve with butter.

BACON-CHEDDAR CORNBREAD

1 cup (125 g) all-purpose flour

1 cup (122 g) yellow cornmeal

½ tsp kosher salt

1 tbsp plus 1 tsp (18 g) baking powder

1 cup (200 g) granulated sugar

1 (15-oz [425-g]) can creamed corn

1 cup (227 g) unsalted butter, melted, plus more for serving

4 eggs

4 slices applewood smoked bacon, cooked until crispy and roughly chopped

1 cup (113 g) shredded cheddar cheese

Spray an 8-inch (20-cm) cake pan, or a pan that will fit inside your insert, with cooking spray. Combine the flour, cornmeal, salt, baking powder and sugar in a mixing bowl. Add the creamed corn, butter, eggs, bacon and cheddar cheese and stir to combine. Add the batter to the prepared pan. Cover with foil. Depending on the size of your Instant Pot you may have to cook the cornbread in two batches.

Place 1 cup (240 ml) of water in the bottom of the Instant Pot insert, add the trivet and place the cake pan on top of it. Seal the lid and turn the valve to the sealing position. Turn the Instant Pot on manual, high pressure for 45 minutes. Release the pressure manually by carefully moving the valve to venting. Carefully remove the cake pan and remove the foil. Cut the cornbread into 8 slices and serve with butter.

CINNAMON-HONEY CORNBREAD

1 cup (125 g) all-purpose flour
1 cup (122 g) yellow cornmeal
½ tsp kosher salt
1 tbsp plus 1 tsp (18 g) baking powder
1 cup (200 g) granulated sugar
1 (15-oz [425-g]) can creamed corn
1 cup (227 g) unsalted butter, melted, plus more for serving
4 eggs
1 tsp ground cinnamon
½ cup (120 ml) honey

Spray an 8-inch (20-cm) cake pan (or a pan that will fit inside your insert) with cooking spray. Combine the flour, cornmeal, salt, baking powder and sugar in a mixing bowl. Add the creamed corn, butter, eggs, cinnamon and honey and stir to combine. Add the batter to the prepared pan. Cover with foil. Depending on the size of your Instant Pot you may have to cook the cornbread in two batches.

Place 1 cup (240 ml) of water in the bottom of the Instant Pot insert, add the trivet and place the cake pan on top of it. Seal the lid and turn the valve to the sealing position. Turn the Instant Pot on manual, high pressure for 45 minutes. Release the pressure manually by carefully moving the valve to venting. Carefully remove the cake pan and remove the foil. Cut the cornbread into 8 slices and serve with butter.

CHORIZO CORNBREAD

1 cup (125 g) all-purpose flour
1 cup (122 g) yellow cornmeal
½ tsp kosher salt
1 tbsp plus 1 tsp (18 g) baking powder
1 cup (200 g) granulated sugar
1 (15-oz [425-g]) can creamed corn
1 cup (226 g) unsalted butter, melted, plus more for serving
4 eggs
1 cup (138 g) pork chorizo, browned and drained of any excess grease

Spray an 8-inch (20-cm) cake pan (or a pan that will fit inside your insert) with cooking spray. Combine the flour, cornmeal, salt, baking powder and sugar in a mixing bowl. Add the creamed corn, butter, eggs and chorizo and stir to combine. Add the batter to the prepared pan. Cover with foil. Depending on the size of your Instant Pot you may have to cook the cornbread in two batches.

Place 1 cup (240 ml) of water in the bottom of the Instant Pot insert, add the trivet and place the cake pan on top of it. Seal the lid and turn the valve to the sealing position. Turn the Instant Pot on manual, high pressure for 45 minutes. Release the pressure manually by carefully moving the valve to venting. Carefully remove the cake pan and remove the foil. Cut the cornbread into 8 slices and serve with butter.

*See image on page 212.

POTATO AU GRATIN

YIELD: 4 SERVINGS

Creamy potatoes au gratin is a rich and cheesy dish. I love serving these potatoes as an easy, but elegant side. I serve the Cinnamon Potato Au Gratin (page 218) for Christmas dinner every year, and everyone is always asking for the secret ingredient.

ORTEGA CHEDDAR

CINNAMON

TRUFFLE

CARAMELIZED ONION AND THYME

ORTEGA CHEDDAR POTATO AU GRATIN

3 tbsp (42 g) unsalted butter
3 tbsp (24 g) all-purpose flour
2 cups (480 ml) milk
1 (4-oz [113-g]) can diced green chilies
3½ cups (396 g) shredded cheddar cheese, divided
1 tsp kosher salt
1 lb (454 g) yellow potatoes, sliced ⅛ inch (3 mm) thick

Preheat a medium-sized saucepan over medium heat. Add the butter to melt. Whisk in the flour and cook for 1 minute. Add the milk and whisk to combine. Bring the mixture to a simmer to thicken. Add the chilies, 2½ cups (283 g) of the cheddar cheese and salt and stir until the cheese is melted.

Spray an 8-inch (20-cm) cake pan (or a pan that will fit inside your insert) with cooking spray. Add a spoonful of the cheese sauce to the bottom of the pan then layer it with a single layer of potatoes. Alternate the cheese sauce and potatoes until you have used up all of the ingredients. Cover with foil.

Add 1 cup (240 ml) of water to the bottom of the Instant Pot insert and add the trivet. Place the cake pan on top of the trivet and seal the lid, making sure the valve is turned to the sealing position. Cook on manual, high pressure for 40 minutes. Manually release the pressure by carefully moving the valve to venting. Carefully remove the cake pan and top the potatoes with the remaining cheese. Place the potatoes under the broiler for 3 to 5 minutes to brown the cheese.

CINNAMON POTATO AU GRATIN

3 tbsp (42 g) unsalted butter
3 tbsp (24 g) all-purpose flour
2 cups (480 ml) milk
¼ tsp ground cinnamon
3½ cups (392 g) shredded Italian five cheese blend, divided
1 tsp kosher salt
½ tsp rosemary, finely chopped
1 lb (454 g) yellow potatoes, sliced ⅛ inch (3 mm) thick

Preheat a medium-sized saucepan over medium heat. Add the butter to melt. Whisk in the flour and cook for 1 minute. Add the milk and whisk to combine. Bring the mixture to a simmer to thicken. Add the cinnamon, 2½ cups (280 g) of the cheese, salt and rosemary and stir until the cheese is melted.

Spray an 8-inch (20-cm) cake pan (or a pan that will fit inside your insert) with cooking spray. Add a spoonful of the cheese sauce to the bottom of the pan then layer it with a single layer of potatoes. Alternate the cheese sauce and potatoes until you have used up all the ingredients. Cover with foil.

Add 1 cup (240 ml) of water to the bottom of the Instant Pot insert and add the trivet. Place the cake pan on top of the trivet and seal the lid, making sure the valve is turned to the sealing position. Cook on manual, high pressure for 40 minutes. Manually release the pressure by carefully moving the valve to venting. Carefully remove the cake pan and top the potatoes with the remaining cheese. Place the potatoes under the broiler for 3 to 5 minutes to brown the cheese.

CARAMELIZED ONION AND THYME POTATO AU GRATIN

3 tbsp (42 g) unsalted butter
½ cup (57 g) white onion, sliced thinly
3 tbsp (24 g) all-purpose flour
2 cups (480 ml) milk
3½ cups (392 g) shredded Italian five cheese blend, divided
1 tsp kosher salt
½ tsp thyme, finely chopped
1 lb (454 g) yellow potatoes, sliced ⅛ inch (3 mm) thick

Preheat a medium-sized saucepan over medium-low heat. Add the butter to melt. Add the onion and cook for 10 minutes, covered. Remove the lid and sauté for 2 minutes, stirring occasionally. Whisk in the flour and cook for 1 minute. Add the milk and whisk to combine. Bring the mixture to a simmer to thicken. Add 2½ cups (280 g) of the cheese blend, salt and thyme and stir until the cheese is melted.

Spray an 8-inch (20-cm) cake pan (or a pan that will fit inside your insert) with cooking spray. Add a spoonful of the cheese sauce to the bottom of the pan then layer it with a single layer of potatoes. Alternate the cheese sauce and potatoes until you have used up all the ingredients. Cover with foil.

Add 1 cup (240 ml) of water to the bottom of the Instant Pot insert and add the trivet. Place the cake pan on top of the trivet and seal the lid, making sure the valve is turned to the sealing position. Cook on manual, high pressure for 40 minutes. Manually release the pressure by carefully moving the valve to venting. Carefully remove the cake pan and top the potatoes with the remaining cheese. Place the potatoes under the broiler for 3 to 5 minutes to brown the cheese.

*See image on page 216.

TRUFFLE POTATO AU GRATIN

2 tbsp (28 g) unsalted butter
1 tbsp (15 g) truffle butter
3 tbsp (24 g) all-purpose flour
2 cups (480 ml) milk
3½ cups (392 g) shredded Italian five cheese blend, divided
1 tsp kosher salt
1 lb (454 g) yellow potatoes, sliced ⅛ inch (3 mm) thick

Preheat a medium-sized saucepan over medium heat. Add the butters to melt. Whisk in flour and cook for 1 minute. Add the milk and whisk to combine. Bring to a simmer to thicken. Add 2½ cups (280 g) of the cheese blend and salt and stir until the cheese is melted.

Spray an 8-inch (20-cm) cake pan (or a pan that will fit inside your insert) with cooking spray. Add a spoonful of the cheese sauce to the bottom of the pan then layer it with a single layer of potatoes. Alternate the cheese sauce and potatoes until you have used up all the ingredients. Cover with foil.

Add 1 cup (240 ml) of water to the bottom of the Instant Pot insert and add the trivet. Place the cake pan on top of the trivet and seal the lid, making sure the valve is turned to the sealing position. Cook on manual, high pressure for 40 minutes. Manually release the pressure by carefully moving the valve to venting. Carefully remove the cake pan and top it with the remaining cheese. Place the potatoes under the broiler for 3 to 5 minutes to brown the cheese.

CORN ON THE COB

YIELD: 6 SERVINGS

Corn on the cob only takes 5 minutes in the Instant Pot. I love making a big batch for BBQs or as a simple side for a quick weeknight dinner. Try out the Chipotle Corn on the Cob (page 223) for a smoky, slightly spicy variation.

ROSEMARY-LEMON

APPLE-CINNAMON

BACON-MAPLE

CHIPOTLE

ROSEMARY-LEMON CORN ON THE COB

6 ears corn, husks and silk removed, cut in half

FOR THE ROSEMARY-LEMON COMPOUND BUTTER

½ cup (114 g) unsalted butter, softened

2 tsp (1 g) fresh rosemary, minced

Zest of 1 lemon

½ tsp kosher salt

Place 1 cup (240 ml) of water in the bottom of the Instant Pot insert and add the steamer basket. Add the corn to the steamer basket. Seal the lid and turn the valve to the sealing position. Turn the Instant Pot on manual, high pressure for 5 minutes. Release the pressure manually by carefully moving the valve to venting. Carefully remove the corn.

Combine the butter, rosemary, lemon zest and salt in a bowl until well combined. Brush the compound butter on top of the corn.

See image on page 220.

APPLE-CINNAMON CORN ON THE COB

6 ears corn, husks and silk removed, cut in half

FOR THE APPLE-CINNAMON COMPOUND BUTTER

½ cup (114 g) unsalted butter, softened

1 tbsp (15 ml) maple syrup

2 tbsp (30 ml) honey

1 tsp ground cinnamon

1 tsp vanilla extract

1 tbsp (15 ml) applesauce

½ tsp kosher salt

Place 1 cup (240 ml) of water in the bottom of the Instant Pot insert and add the steamer basket. Add the corn to the steamer basket. Seal the lid and turn the valve to the sealing position. Turn the Instant Pot on manual, high pressure for 5 minutes. Release the pressure manually by carefully moving the valve to venting. Carefully remove the corn.

Combine the butter, syrup, honey, cinnamon, vanilla, applesauce and salt in a bowl until well combined. Brush the compound butter on top of the corn.

CHIPOTLE CORN ON THE COB

6 ears corn, husks and silk removed, cut in half

FOR THE CHIPOTLE COMPOUND BUTTER
½ cup (114 g) unsalted butter, softened
1 tbsp (15 ml) honey
1 tsp chipotle in adobo sauce
½ tsp kosher salt

Place 1 cup (240 ml) of water in the bottom of the Instant Pot insert and add the steamer basket. Add the corn to the steamer basket. Seal the lid and turn the valve to the sealing position. Turn the Instant Pot on manual, high pressure for 5 minutes. Release the pressure manually by carefully moving the valve to venting. Carefully remove the corn.

Combine the butter, honey, chipotle and salt in a bowl until well combined. Brush the compound butter on top of the corn.

BACON-MAPLE CORN ON THE COB

6 ears corn, husks and silk removed, cut in half

FOR THE BACON-MAPLE COMPOUND BUTTER
½ cup (114 g) unsalted butter, softened
2 tsp (10 ml) maple syrup
½ tsp kosher salt
2 tbsp (40 g) applewood smoked bacon, cooked until crispy and finely chopped

Place 1 cup (240 ml) of water in the bottom of the Instant Pot insert and add the steamer basket. Add the corn to the steamer basket. Seal the lid and turn the valve to the sealing position. Turn the Instant Pot on manual, high pressure for 5 minutes. Release the pressure manually by carefully moving the valve to venting. Carefully remove the corn.

Combine the butter, syrup, salt and bacon in a bowl until well combined. Brush the compound butter on top of the corn.

CARROTS

YIELD: 5 SERVINGS

Carrots are a quick side in the Instant Pot. I love pressure cooking them first and then turning the pot on to sauté mode to get a little caramelization. The kids especially love the Maple-Glazed Carrots (page 226). They are slightly sweet and tender.

PISTACHIO—GOAT CHEESE

MAPLE-GLAZED

CRANBERRY-ORANGE

ROSEMARY-THYME

MAPLE-GLAZED CARROTS

2 lbs (907 g) carrots, peeled and cut on a ½-inch (1.3-cm) bias
⅓ cup (80 ml) water
1 tsp kosher salt
2 tbsp (28 g) unsalted butter
2 tbsp (30 ml) maple syrup

Place the carrots, water and salt into the Instant Pot insert. Seal the lid and move the valve to the sealing position. Cook on manual, high pressure for 1 minute. Naturally release the pressure for 5 minutes. Drain any excess liquid and turn the pot on to sauté mode. Add the butter and maple syrup and sauté for 5 minutes to caramelize.

CRANBERRY-ORANGE CARROTS

2 lbs (907 g) carrots, peeled and cut on a ½-inch (1.3-cm) bias
⅓ cup (80 ml) water
1 tsp kosher salt
2 tbsp (30 ml) maple syrup
2 tbsp (28 g) unsalted butter
Zest of 1 orange
2 tbsp (14 g) dried cranberries

Place the carrots, water and salt into the Instant Pot insert. Seal the lid and move the valve to the sealing position. Cook on manual, high pressure for 1 minute. Naturally release the pressure for 5 minutes. Drain any excess liquid and turn the pot on to sauté mode. Add the syrup, butter, orange zest and cranberries and sauté for 5 minutes.

ROSEMARY-THYME CARROTS

2 lbs (907 g) carrots, peeled and cut on a ½-inch (1.3-cm) bias

⅓ cup (80 ml) water

1 tsp kosher salt

2 tbsp (28 g) unsalted butter

2 tsp (1 g) rosemary, finely chopped

1 tsp thyme, finely chopped

Place the carrots, water and salt into the Instant Pot insert. Seal the lid and move the valve to the sealing position. Cook on manual, high pressure for 1 minute. Naturally release the pressure for 5 minutes. Drain any excess liquid and turn the pot on to sauté mode. Add the butter, rosemary and thyme and sauté for 5 minutes.

PISTACHIO-GOAT CHEESE CARROTS

2 lbs (907 g) carrots, peeled and cut on a ½-inch (1.3-cm) bias

⅓ cup (80 ml) water

1 tsp kosher salt

2 tbsp (28 g) unsalted butter

1 tbsp (7 g) pistachios, finely chopped

¼ cup (56 g) honey goat cheese, crumbled

Place the carrots, water and salt into the Instant Pot insert. Seal the lid and move the valve to the sealing position. Cook on manual, high pressure for 1 minute. Naturally release the pressure for 5 minutes. Drain any excess liquid and turn the pot on to sauté mode. Add the butter and sauté for 5 minutes. Remove the carrots and top them with the pistachios and goat cheese.

See image on page 224.

DESSERT

The first dessert I made in the Instant Pot was a molten lava cake. They came out perfectly, and I would say even better than when I cooked them in the oven! The Instant Pot takes dessert to a whole new level, my friends. Moist, perfectly cooked desserts can be made in the Instant Pot quickly and easily without having to worry about burning anything.

Just make sure to use a separate, designated dessert sealing ring so your dessert doesn't taste like last night's curry dish.

I can't wait for you to make some desserts in your Instant Pot. The molten Lava Cakes (page 235) remain my all-time favorite Instant Pot dessert. You can fill them with a variety of fillings like peanut butter, Biscoff butter or my favorite filling, Nutella™.

CHEESECAKE BITES

YIELD: 35–40 CHEESECAKE BITES

Cheesecake bites are the perfect party food. People can grab one of each flavor without having to eat a whole piece of cheesecake. Make sure you try out the Cookie Dough Cheesecake Bites (page 232) if you have to choose one. They are rich, creamy and deliciously decadent.

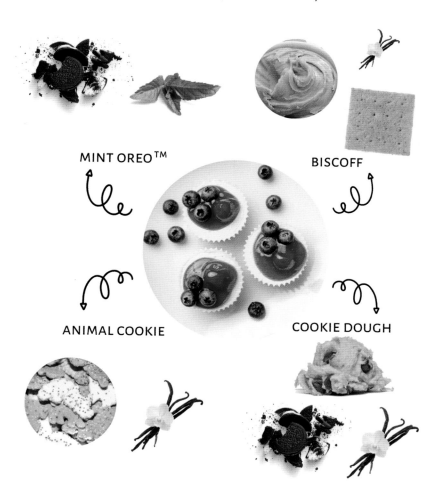

MINT OREO™

BISCOFF

ANIMAL COOKIE

COOKIE DOUGH

MINT OREO™ CHEESECAKE BITES

FOR THE CRUST

8 mint Oreo™ cookies
3 tbsp (42 g) unsalted butter, melted

FOR THE FILLING

1 lb (454 g) cream cheese, at room temperature
½ cup (100 g) granulated sugar
2 eggs
1 tsp mint extract
1 cup (134 g) mint Oreo™ cookies, roughly chopped

Spray a silicone mini muffin mold with cooking spray.

To make the crust, place the cookies in a food processor and pulse until they become fine crumbs. Stir in the melted butter and set aside.

Make the filling by placing the cream cheese and granulated sugar in a stand mixer fitted with a paddle attachment and mixing on medium-low to combine. Add one egg at a time and then add the mint extract. Stir in the Oreos™ by hand.

Add 1½ teaspoons (10 g) of the crust mixture to each mold and press down with your thumb to create a firm layer. Fill each mold with 2 teaspoons (15 g) of filling, cover with a paper towel and then cover with foil.

Add 1 cup (240 ml) of water to the Instant Pot and add a trivet. Place the mold on the trivet and seal the lid, making sure the valve is in the sealing position. Cook on manual, high pressure for 4 minutes. Let the pressure release naturally for 10 minutes. Remove the mold and let it cool at room temperature for 10 minutes. Remove the cheesecake bites carefully from the mold and place them in the refrigerator to chill for at least 2 hours.

See image on page 230.

COOKIE DOUGH CHEESECAKE BITES

FOR THE CRUST

8 Oreo™ cookies
3 tbsp (42 g) unsalted butter, melted

FOR THE FILLING

1 lb (454 g) cream cheese, at room temperature
½ cup (100 g) granulated sugar
2 eggs
1 tsp vanilla extract
1 cup (224 g) premade cookie dough, crumbled

Spray a silicone mini muffin mold with cooking spray.

To make the crust, place the cookies in a food processor and pulse until they become fine crumbs. Stir in the melted butter and set aside.

Make the filling by placing the cream cheese and granulated sugar in a stand mixer fitted with a paddle attachment and mixing on medium-low to combine. Add one egg at a time and then add the vanilla. Stir in the cookie dough crumbles by hand.

Add 1½ teaspoons (10 g) of the crust mixture to each mold and press down with your thumb to create a firm layer. Fill each mold with 2 teaspoons (15 g) of the filling, cover with a paper towel and then cover with foil.

Add 1 cup (240 ml) of water to the Instant Pot and add a trivet. Place the mold on the trivet and seal the lid, making sure the valve is in the sealing position. Cook on manual, high pressure for 4 minutes. Let the pressure release naturally for 10 minutes. Remove the mold and let it cool at room temperature for 10 minutes. Remove the cheesecake bites carefully from the mold and place them in the refrigerator to chill for at least 2 hours.

ANIMAL COOKIE CHEESECAKE BITES

FOR THE CRUST

1 cup (55 g) iced animal cookies
3 tbsp (42 g) unsalted butter, melted

FOR THE FILLING

1 lb (454 g) cream cheese, at room temperature
½ cup (100 g) granulated sugar
2 eggs
1 tsp vanilla extract
1 cup (55 g) iced animal cookies, roughly chopped

Spray a silicone mini muffin mold with cooking spray.

To make the crust, place the cookies in a food processor and pulse until they become fine crumbs. Stir in the melted butter and set aside.

Make the filling by placing the cream cheese and granulated sugar in a stand mixer fitted with a paddle attachment and mixing on medium-low to combine. Add one egg at a time and then add the vanilla. Stir in the animal cookies by hand.

Add 1½ teaspoons (10 g) of the crust mixture to each mold and press down with your thumb to create a firm layer. Fill each mold with 2 teaspoons (15 g) of the filling, cover with a paper towel and then cover with foil.

Add 1 cup (240 ml) of water to the Instant Pot and add a trivet. Place the mold on the trivet and seal the lid, making sure the valve is in the sealing position. Cook on manual, high pressure for 4 minutes. Let the pressure release naturally for 10 minutes. Remove the mold and let it cool at room temperature for 10 minutes. Remove the cheesecake bites carefully from the mold and place them in the refrigerator to chill for at least 2 hours.

BISCOFF CHEESECAKE BITES

FOR THE CRUST

5 graham crackers
3 tbsp (42 g) unsalted butter, melted

FOR THE FILLING

1 lb (454 g) cream cheese, at room temperature
½ cup (100 g) granulated sugar
2 eggs
1 tsp vanilla extract
¼ cup (60 g) Biscoff cookie butter

Spray a silicone mini muffin mold with cooking spray.

To make the crust, place the graham crackers in a food processor and pulse until they become fine crumbs. Stir in the melted butter and set aside.

Make the filling by placing the cream cheese and granulated sugar in a stand mixer fitted with a paddle attachment and mixing on medium-low to combine. Add one egg at a time. Then add the vanilla and cookie butter, mixing to combine.

Add 1½ teaspoons (10 g) of the crust mixture to each mold and press down with your thumb to create a firm layer. Fill each mold with 2 teaspoons (15 g) of the filling, cover with a paper towel and then cover with foil.

Add 1 cup (240 ml) of water to the Instant Pot and add a trivet. Place the mold on the trivet and seal the lid, making sure the valve is in the sealing position. Cook on manual, high pressure for 4 minutes. Let the pressure release naturally for 10 minutes. Remove the mold and let it cool at room temperature for 10 minutes. Remove the cheesecake bites carefully from the mold and place them in the refrigerator to chill for at least 2 hours.

LAVA CAKES

YIELD: 4 LAVA CAKES

Molten lava cakes are rich, gooey in the middle and the perfect dessert for a fancy dinner party. The best part is that you can flavor the cakes with a variety of flavors. My all-time favorite is the Peanut Butter Lava Cake (page 236). It's rich and chocolaty with a molten peanut butter filling. These delicious cakes are made even tastier when you serve them with vanilla ice cream and chocolate sauce.

MINT CHOCOLATE

BISCOFF

PEANUT BUTTER

NUTELLA™

MINT CHOCOLATE LAVA CAKES

¾ cup (170 g) unsalted butter, divided
4½ oz (127 g) dark chocolate, chopped fine
1 cup (120 g) powdered sugar
2 whole eggs
2 egg yolks
1 tsp mint extract
3 tbsp (24 g) all-purpose flour
2 tbsp (11 g) dark cocoa powder (for dusting)

Melt ½ cup (114 g) of the butter in a small, microwave-safe bowl. Add the chocolate and stir until the chocolate is melted. Place the chocolate and butter mixture into a mixing bowl and add the powdered sugar. Stir to combine. Add the eggs and yolks one at a time, stirring in between to combine completely before adding the next egg. Add the mint extract and flour and stir to combine.

Smear a thin layer of the remaining butter in each of four 8-ounce (240-ml) ramekins, then add the cocoa powder and rotate to coat. Remove any excess cocoa powder. Fill the ramekins two-thirds full with batter. Add 1 cup (240 ml) of water to the Instant Pot and add a trivet. Place the ramekins on the trivet.

Seal the lid and move the valve to the sealing position. Cook on manual, high pressure for 9 minutes. Manually release the pressure by carefully moving the valve to the venting position. Let the cakes cool for 3 minutes. Run a knife along the sides of the cakes and invert onto a plate.

PEANUT BUTTER LAVA CAKES

¾ cup (170 g) unsalted butter, divided
4½ oz (127 g) dark chocolate, chopped fine
1 cup (120 g) powdered sugar
2 whole eggs
2 egg yolks
1 tsp vanilla extract
3 tbsp (24 g) all-purpose flour
2 tbsp (11 g) dark cocoa powder (for dusting)

FOR THE PEANUT BUTTER FILLING

4 tbsp (64 g) peanut butter
1 tbsp (14 g) unsalted butter, softened
2 tbsp (16 g) powdered sugar

Melt ½ cup (114 g) of the butter in a small, microwave-safe bowl. Add the chocolate and stir until the chocolate is melted. Place the chocolate and butter mixture into a mixing bowl and add the powdered sugar. Stir to combine. Add the eggs and yolks one at a time, stirring in between to combine completely before adding the next egg. Add the vanilla and flour and stir to combine.

Smear a thin layer of the remaining butter in each of four 8-ounce (240-ml) ramekins, then add the cocoa powder and rotate to coat. Remove any excess cocoa powder. Fill the ramekins one-third full with batter, reserving the rest of the batter. In a small bowl combine the peanut butter, butter and powdered sugar and place 1 teaspoon of the filling in the center of each ramekin. Divide the remaining batter evenly between the four ramekins so that they are filled two-thirds of the way. Add 1 cup (240 ml) of water to the Instant Pot and add a trivet. Place the ramekins on the trivet.

Seal the lid and move the valve to the sealing position. Cook on manual, high pressure for 9 minutes. Manually release the pressure by carefully moving the valve to the venting position. Let the cakes cool for 3 minutes. Run a knife along the sides of the cakes and invert onto a plate.

BISCOFF LAVA CAKES

¾ cup (170 g) unsalted butter, divided

4½ oz (127 g) dark chocolate, chopped fine

1 cup (120 g) powdered sugar

2 whole eggs

2 egg yolks

1 tsp vanilla extract

3 tbsp (24 g) all-purpose flour

2 tbsp (11 g) dark cocoa powder, for dusting

FOR THE BISCOFF FILLING

4 tbsp (60 g) Biscoff cookie butter

1 tbsp (14 g) unsalted butter, softened

2 tbsp (16 g) powdered sugar

Melt ½ cup (114 g) of the butter in a small, microwave-safe bowl. Add the chocolate and stir until the chocolate is melted. Place the chocolate and butter mixture into a mixing bowl and add the powdered sugar. Stir to combine. Add the eggs and yolks one at a time, stirring in between to combine completely before adding the next egg. Add the vanilla and flour and stir to combine.

Smear a thin layer of the remaining butter in each of four 8-ounce (240-ml) ramekins, then add the cocoa powder and rotate to coat. Remove any excess cocoa powder. Fill the ramekins one-third full with batter, reserving the rest of the batter. In a small bowl combine the cookie butter, butter and powdered sugar and place 1 teaspoon of the filling in the center of each ramekin. Divide the remaining batter evenly between the four ramekins so that they are filled two-thirds of the way. Add 1 cup (240 ml) of water to the Instant Pot and add a trivet. Place the ramekins on the trivet.

Seal the lid and move the valve to the sealing position. Cook on manual, high pressure for 9 minutes. Manually release the pressure by carefully moving the valve to the venting position. Let the cakes cool for 3 minutes. Run a knife along the sides of the cakes and invert onto a plate.

NUTELLA™ LAVA CAKES

¾ cup (170 g) unsalted butter, divided

4½ oz (127 g) dark chocolate, chopped fine

1 cup (120 g) powdered sugar

2 whole eggs

2 egg yolks

1 tsp vanilla extract

3 tbsp (24 g) all-purpose flour

2 tbsp (11 g) dark cocoa powder (for dusting)

FOR THE NUTELLA™ FILLING

4 tbsp (74 g) Nutella™

1 tbsp (14 g) unsalted butter, softened

2 tbsp (16 g) powdered sugar

Melt ½ cup (114 g) of the butter in a small, microwave-safe bowl. Add the chocolate and stir until the chocolate is melted. Place the chocolate and butter mixture into a mixing bowl and add the powdered sugar. Stir to combine. Add the eggs and yolks one at a time, stirring in between to combine completely before adding the next egg. Add the vanilla and flour and stir to combine.

Smear a thin layer of the remaining butter in each of four 8-ounce (240-ml) ramekins, then add the cocoa powder and rotate to coat. Remove any excess cocoa powder. Fill the ramekins one-third full with batter, reserving the rest of the batter. In a small bowl combine the Nutella™, butter and powdered sugar and place 1 teaspoon of the filling in the center of each ramekin. Divide the remaining batter evenly between the four ramekins so that they are filled two-thirds of the way. Add 1 cup (240 ml) of water to the Instant Pot and add a trivet. Place the ramekins on the trivet.

Seal the lid and move the valve to the sealing position. Cook on manual, high pressure for 9 minutes. Manually release the pressure by carefully moving the valve to the venting position. Let the cakes cool for 3 minutes. Run a knife along the sides of the cakes and invert onto a plate.

See image on page 234.

POKE CAKE

Cake is one of my favorite desserts to make in the Instant Pot because they come out so moist and cook evenly every time. This recipe yields two cakes. You can make two individual cakes, make a trifle or make a two-layered cake with these poke cake ideas.

LEMON-RASPBERRY

PUMPKIN-TOFFEE

CHOCOLATE TURTLE

CREAM PUFF

LEMON-RASPBERRY POKE CAKE

1 (15.25-oz [432-g]) box white cake mix
1 (3.4-oz [96-g]) box lemon pudding mix
½ cup (120 ml) vegetable oil
1 cup (240 ml) water
3 eggs
½ cup (120 ml) raspberry jam, warmed
1 (8-oz [226-g]) container whipped topping, such as Cool Whip
1 cup (123 g) fresh raspberries

Spray 2 cake pans that fit within your Instant Pot insert with cooking spray. In a medium-sized mixing bowl, combine the cake mix, pudding mix, oil, water and eggs. Fill each pan equally with cake batter. Cover the pans with a paper towel and then with foil.

Add 1 cup (240 ml) of water into the Instant Pot insert and add the trivet. Place one cake on the trivet. Form a foil trivet by scrunching up a 12-inch (30-cm) piece of foil. Place it on top of the cake that is in the pot, then top with the remaining cake. Cover with the lid and move the valve to the sealing position. Cook on manual, high pressure for 30 minutes. Manually release the pressure by carefully moving the valve to the venting position.

Remove the cakes and poke holes with the tip of a straw or a fork into the entire surface of each cake. Top with warm jam and let cool. Once the cakes are cool, top them with the whipped topping and fresh raspberries.

PUMPKIN-TOFFEE POKE CAKE

1 (15.25-oz [432-g]) box spice cake mix
½ cup (120 ml) oil
1 cup (240 ml) water
3 eggs
1 (3.4-oz [96-g]) box vanilla pudding mix
¼ cup (55 g) pumpkin puree
1 (8-oz [226-g]) container whipped topping, such as Cool Whip
Toffee bits, for garnish
Caramel sauce, for garnish

Spray 2 cake pans that fit within your Instant Pot insert with cooking spray. In a medium-sized mixing bowl, combine the cake mix with the oil, water and eggs. Fill each pan equally with cake batter. Cover the pans with a paper towel and then with foil.

Add 1 cup (240 ml) of water into the Instant Pot insert and add the trivet. Place one cake on the trivet. Form a foil trivet by scrunching up a 12-inch (30-cm) piece of foil. Place it on top of the cake that is in the pot, then top with the remaining cake. Cover with the lid and move the valve to the sealing position. Cook on manual, high pressure for 30 minutes. Meanwhile, make the vanilla pudding according to the package directions and add the pumpkin puree. Let the pudding set in the refrigerator. Manually release the pressure by carefully moving the valve to the venting position.

Remove the cakes and poke holes with the tip of a straw or a fork into the entire surface of each cake. Top with the pudding and place them in the fridge. Once the cakes are cool, top them with the whipped topping, toffee bits and a drizzle of caramel sauce.

CHOCOLATE TURTLE POKE CAKE

1 (15.25-oz [432-g]) box chocolate cake mix
1 (3.4-oz [96-g]) box chocolate pudding mix
½ cup (120 ml) oil
1 cup (240 ml) water
3 eggs
½ cup (120 ml) chocolate sauce
1 cup (112 g) pretzels
½ cup (120 ml) caramel sauce

Spray 2 cake pans that fit within your Instant Pot insert with cooking spray. In a medium-sized mixing bowl, combine the cake mix, pudding mix, oil, water and eggs. Fill each pan equally with cake batter. Cover the pan with a paper towel and then with foil.

Place 1 cup (240 ml) of water into the Instant pot insert and add the trivet. Place one cake on the trivet. Form a foil trivet by scrunching up a 12-inch (30-cm) piece of foil. Place it on top of the cake that is in the pot, then top with the remaining cake. Cover with the lid and move the valve to the sealing position. Cook on manual, high pressure for 30 minutes. Manually release the pressure by carefully moving the valve to the venting position.

Remove and poke holes with a tip of a straw or with a fork into the entire surface of each cake. Top with chocolate sauce and let cool. Once the cakes are cool, top them with the pretzels and caramel sauce.

See image on page 238.

CREAM PUFF POKE CAKE

1 (15.25-oz [432-g]) box yellow cake mix
½ cup (120 ml) oil
1 cup (240 ml) water
3 eggs
1 (3.4-oz [96-g]) box vanilla pudding mix
1 (8-oz [226-g]) container of whipped topping, such as Cool Whip
Chocolate sauce, for garnish

Spray 2 cake pans that fit within your Instant Pot insert with cooking spray. In a medium-sized mixing bowl, combine the cake mix, oil, water and eggs. Fill each pan equally with cake batter. Cover the pan with a paper towel and then with foil.

Add 1 cup (240 ml) of water into the Instant Pot insert and add the trivet. Place one cake on the trivet. Form a foil trivet by scrunching up a 12-inch (30-cm) piece of foil. Place it on top of the cake that is in the pot, then top with the remaining cake. Cover with the lid and move the valve to the sealing position. Cook on manual, high pressure for 30 minutes. Meanwhile make the vanilla pudding according to the package directions and let it set in the refrigerator. Manually release the pressure by carefully moving the valve to the venting position.

Remove and poke holes with the tip of a straw or with a fork into the entire surface of each cake. Let the cakes cool for 10 minutes. Top with pudding and place them in the fridge. Once the cakes are cool, top them with the whipped topping and a drizzle of chocolate sauce.

BROWNIES

YIELD: 6 SERVINGS

Instant Pot brownies are perfectly moist and fudgy. Feel free to top them with any of your favorite toppings. The Peppermint Brownies (page 245) have become a Christmas tradition in our family. They are always a huge hit.

PEPPERMINT

MEXICAN HOT CHOCOLATE

RASPBERRY CHEESECAKE

COOKIE DOUGH

COOKIE DOUGH BROWNIES

½ cup (114 g) unsalted butter
⅔ cup (132 g) granulated sugar
2 tbsp (30 ml) water
1 cup (224 g) semi-sweet chocolate chips
2 eggs
1 tsp vanilla extract
½ tsp baking soda
1⅓ cups (166 g) all-purpose flour
¼ cup (56 g) chocolate chip cookie dough, crumbled

Place the butter, sugar and water into a saucepan over low heat. Stir to combine until the butter is completely melted. Add the chocolate chips and stir until they have melted. Take the mixture off the heat. Add the eggs and vanilla extract and stir until completely incorporated. Add the baking soda and flour, stirring to combine.

Spray an Instant Pot springform pan with cooking spray and fill it with the brownie batter. Top with the crumbled cookie dough and cover with foil. Fill the Instant Pot insert with 1 cup (240 ml) of water. Add a high trivet and top it with the springform pan. Seal the lid and turn the valve to the sealing position. Turn the Instant Pot on manual, high pressure for 45 minutes. Release the pressure manually by carefully moving the valve to venting. Remove the pan and foil and let the brownies cool for 5 minutes. Run a knife along the side of the pan and release the pan. Slice into 6 individual slices.

MEXICAN HOT CHOCOLATE BROWNIES

½ cup (114 g) unsalted butter
⅔ cup (132 g) granulated sugar
2 tbsp (30 ml) water
1 cup (224 g) semi-sweet chocolate chips
2 eggs
1 tsp vanilla extract
½ tsp ground cinnamon
⅛ tsp cayenne pepper
½ tsp baking soda
1⅓ cups (166 g) all-purpose flour

Place the butter, sugar and water into a saucepan over low heat. Stir to combine until the butter is completely melted. Add the chocolate chips and stir until they have melted. Take the mixture off the heat. Add the eggs, vanilla, cinnamon and cayenne pepper and stir until completely incorporated. Add the baking soda and flour, stirring to combine.

Spray an Instant Pot springform pan with cooking spray and fill it with the brownie batter. Cover the pan with foil. Fill the Instant Pot insert with 1 cup (240 ml) of water. Add a high trivet and top it with the springform pan. Seal the lid and turn the valve to the sealing position. Turn the Instant Pot on manual, high pressure for 45 minutes. Release the pressure manually by carefully moving the valve to venting. Remove the pan and foil and let the brownies cool for 5 minutes. Run a knife along the side of the pan and release the pan. Slice into 6 individual slices.

PEPPERMINT BROWNIES

½ cup (114 g) unsalted butter

⅔ cup (132 g) granulated sugar

2 tbsp (30 ml) water

1 cup (224 g) semi-sweet chocolate chips

2 eggs

1 tsp peppermint extract

½ tsp baking soda

1⅓ cups (166 g) all-purpose flour

1 cup (43 g) peppermint bark candy, roughly chopped

Place the butter, sugar and water into a saucepan over low heat. Stir to combine until the butter is completely melted. Add the chocolate chips and stir until they have melted. Take the mixture off the heat. Add the eggs and peppermint extract and stir until completely incorporated. Add the baking soda and flour, stirring to combine.

Spray an Instant Pot springform pan with cooking spray and fill it with the brownie batter. Cover the pan with foil. Fill the Instant Pot insert with 1 cup (240 ml) of water. Add a high trivet and top it with the springform pan. Seal the lid and turn the valve to the sealing position. Turn the Instant Pot on manual, high pressure for 45 minutes. Release the pressure manually by carefully moving the valve to venting. Remove the pan and foil and immediately top it with peppermint bark candy and let the brownies cool for 5 minutes. Run a knife along the side of the pan and release the pan. Slice into 6 individual slices.

RASPBERRY CHEESECAKE BROWNIES

½ cup (114 g) unsalted butter

⅔ cup plus ¼ cup (182 g) granulated sugar, divided

2 tbsp (30 ml) water

1 cup (224 g) semi-sweet chocolate chips

3 eggs, divided

1 tsp vanilla extract

½ tsp baking soda

1⅓ cups (166 g) all-purpose flour

8 oz (226 g) cream cheese, at room temperature

¼ cup (60 ml) raspberry jam

Place the butter, ⅔ cup (132 g) of sugar and water into a saucepan over low heat and stir to combine until the butter is melted. Add the chocolate chips and stir until they have melted. Take the mixture off the heat. Stir in 2 eggs and the vanilla. Add the baking soda and flour, stirring to combine. Spray an Instant Pot springform pan with cooking spray and fill it with the brownie batter.

To make the cheesecake, cream together the cream cheese and remaining ¼ cup (50 g) of sugar using a stand mixer. Add the remaining egg and mix until well combined. Top the brownie batter with the cheesecake batter. Place dollops of raspberry jam throughout the cheesecake batter. With a toothpick, swirl the jam throughout the cheese-cake batter. Cover with foil.

Fill the Instant Pot insert with 1 cup (240 ml) of water. Add a high trivet and top it with the springform pan. Seal the lid and turn the valve to the sealing position. Turn the Instant Pot on manual, high pressure for 50 minutes. Release the pressure manually by carefully moving the valve to venting. Remove the pan and refrigerate for at least 1 hour. Run a knife along the side of the pan and release the pan. Slice into 6 individual slices.

See image on page 242.

CHURRO BITES

YIELD: 12 BITES

I love serving these mini churro bites for Mexican-inspired events or get-togethers. You can make all the flavors and serve them as a churro bar. Include some fun syrups, toppings and even ice cream. The Strawberry Churro Bites (page 249) are my all-time favorite.

OREO™

CINNAMON-SUGAR

LEMON

STRAWBERRY

CINNAMON-SUGAR CHURRO BITES

½ cup (110 g) brown sugar
½ cup (114 g) unsalted butter, melted
½ cup (120 ml) milk
1 tsp baking powder
½ tsp baking soda
1 cup (125 g) all-purpose flour

FOR THE COATING

½ cup (114 g) unsalted butter, melted
1 cup (200 g) granulated sugar mixed with 2 tsp (5 g) ground cinnamon

Spray a silicone Instant Pot mini muffin mold with cooking spray. Combine the brown sugar, butter, milk, baking powder, baking soda and flour in a mixing bowl. Fill the prepared mold three-fourths of the way with batter. Cover with a paper towel and then with foil. Place 1 cup (240 ml) of water into the Instant Pot, add a trivet and top it with the mold. Seal the lid and turn the valve to the sealing position.

Turn the Instant Pot on manual, high pressure for 12 minutes. Let the pressure release naturally for 10 minutes. Let it cool for 5 minutes. Remove the churro bites from the mold and dip them in the melted butter. Toss the bites in the cinnamon-sugar to coat.

See image on page 246.

OREO™ CHURRO BITES

½ cup (110 g) brown sugar
½ cup (114 g) unsalted butter, melted
½ cup (120 ml) milk
1 tsp baking powder
½ tsp baking soda
1 cup (125 g) all-purpose flour
10 Oreos™, ground into fine crumbs, divided

FOR THE COATING

½ cup (114 g) unsalted butter, melted
Leftover cookie crumbs from batter

Spray a silicone Instant Pot mini muffin mold with cooking spray. Combine the brown sugar, butter, milk, baking powder, baking soda, flour and 3 tablespoons (17 g) of Oreo™ crumbs in a mixing bowl. Fill the prepared mold three-fourths of the way with batter. Cover with a paper towel and then with foil. Place 1 cup (240 ml) of water into the Instant Pot, add a trivet and top it with the mold. Seal the lid and turn the valve to the sealing position.

Turn the Instant Pot on manual, high pressure for 12 minutes. Let the pressure release naturally for 10 minutes. Let the mold cool for 5 minutes. Remove the churro bites from the mold and dip them in the melted butter. Toss the bites in the remaining crumbs to coat.

STRAWBERRY CHURRO BITES

½ cup (110 g) brown sugar
½ cup (114 g) unsalted butter, melted
½ cup (120 ml) milk
1 tsp baking powder
½ tsp baking soda
1 cup (125 g) all-purpose flour
¼ cup (45 g) strawberries, mashed

FOR THE COATING

1 cup (200 g) granulated sugar
¼ cup (4 g) freeze-dried strawberries, crushed into fine crumbs
½ cup (114 g) unsalted butter, melted

Spray a silicone Instant Pot mini muffin mold with cooking spray. Combine the brown sugar, butter, milk, baking powder, baking soda, flour and strawberries in a mixing bowl. Fill the prepared mold three-fourths of the way with batter. Cover with a paper towel and then with foil. Place 1 cup (240 ml) of water into the Instant Pot, add a trivet and top it with the mold. Seal the lid and turn the valve to the sealing position.

Turn the Instant Pot on manual, high pressure for 12 minutes. Let the pressure release naturally for 10 minutes. Let the mold cool for 5 minutes. In a bowl, combine the sugar and strawberry crumbs. Remove the churro bites from the mold and dip in the melted butter. Toss the bites in the strawberries to coat.

LEMON CHURRO BITES

½ cup (110 g) brown sugar
½ cup (114 g) unsalted butter, melted
½ cup (120 ml) milk
1 tsp baking powder
½ tsp baking soda
1 cup (125 g) all-purpose flour
Zest of 2 lemons

FOR THE COATING

1 cup (200 g) granulated sugar
Zest of 2 lemons
½ cup (114 g) unsalted butter, melted

FOR THE GLAZE

½ cup (60 g) powdered sugar
1–2 tsp (5–10 ml) lemon juice

Spray a silicone Instant Pot mini muffin mold with cooking spray. Combine the brown sugar, butter, milk, baking powder, baking soda, flour and lemon zest in a mixing bowl. Fill the prepared mold three-fourths of the way with batter. Cover with a paper towel and then with foil. Place 1 cup (240 ml) of water into the Instant Pot, add a trivet and top it with the mold. Seal the lid and turn the valve to the sealing position.

Turn the Instant Pot on manual, high pressure for 12 minutes. Let the pressure release naturally for 10 minutes. Let the mold cool for 5 minutes. For the coating combine the sugar and lemon zest in a bowl. In another bowl, combine the powdered sugar and lemon juice. Remove the churro bites from the mold and dip them in the melted butter. Toss in the lemon sugar to coat and drizzle the glaze over the churro bites.

BREAD PUDDING

YIELD: 6 SERVINGS

Bread pudding was something we had growing up and I loved how decadent it tasted. Making bread pudding in the Instant Pot is my new favorite method. It stays moist and delicious and doesn't dry out. I love to serve bread pudding warm with some ice cream or whipped cream on top.

PIÑA COLADA

PEACH CRUMBLE

BANANA CREAM PIE

CINNAMON ROLL

PIÑA COLADA BREAD PUDDING

3 eggs
1 (13.6-oz [402-ml]) can coconut milk
½ cup (100 g) granulated sugar
6 cups (210 g) Hawaiian bread, diced into 1-inch (3-cm) cubes, left out overnight
1 cup (165 g) fresh or canned pineapple, diced
6 maraschino cherries

FOR THE SAUCE

1 (14-oz [397-g]) can sweetened condensed milk
1 tsp pure coconut extract
¼ tsp butter extract
Pinch of salt

Place the eggs, coconut milk and sugar in a mixing bowl and whisk to combine. Add the stale bread and pineapple and stir to combine, being careful not to break the bread up too much.

Spray an Instant Pot springform pan with cooking spray, then fill it with the bread mixture and cover with foil. Fill the Instant Pot insert with 1 cup (240 ml) of water. Add a high trivet and top it with the springform pan. Seal the lid and turn the valve to the sealing position. Turn the Instant Pot on manual, high pressure for 45 minutes. Release the pressure manually by carefully moving the valve to venting. Remove the pan and foil and let it cool for 5 minutes.

Combine the condensed milk, extracts and salt in a small saucepan over medium heat and stir for 5 minutes, or until the sauce is warmed through. Slice the bread pudding into 6 individual slices and top each slice with sauce and a maraschino cherry.

See image on page 250.

PEACH CRUMBLE BREAD PUDDING

1 cup (240 ml) whole milk
3 eggs
½ cup (110 g) brown sugar
½ tsp cinnamon
1 (15-oz [425-g]) can peaches, drained
6 cups (210 g) Brioche, diced into 1-inch (3-cm) cubes, left out overnight

FOR THE TOPPING

1 cup (125 g) all-purpose flour
½ cup (110 g) brown sugar
¼ tsp cinnamon
5 tbsp (70 g) unsalted butter, diced

Place the milk, eggs, brown sugar and cinnamon in a mixing bowl and whisk to combine. Add the peaches and stale bread and carefully stir to combine, being careful not to break the bread up too much. In another bowl, combine the flour, brown sugar and cinnamon and cut the butter into the mixture until it looks like a coarse wet sand.

Spray an Instant Pot springform pan with cooking spray and fill it with the bread mixture. Top it with the crumb topping and cover with foil. Fill the Instant Pot insert with 1 cup (240 ml) of water. Add a high trivet and top it with the springform pan. Seal the lid and turn the valve to the sealing position. Turn the Instant Pot on manual, high pressure for 40 minutes. Release the pressure manually by carefully moving the valve to venting. Remove the pan and foil and let cool for 5 minutes. Cut the bread pudding into 6 slices.

BANANA CREAM PIE BREAD PUDDING

3 eggs
2 cups (480 ml) whole milk, divided
½ cup (100 g) granulated sugar
1 (3.4-oz [96-g]) box dry banana pudding mix, divided
6 cups (210 g) Hawaiian bread, diced into 1-inch (3-cm) cubes (left out overnight)
2 sliced bananas, for topping
Whipped cream, for serving (optional)

Place the eggs, 1 cup (240 ml) of the milk, the sugar and ¼ cup (about 50 g) of the dry banana pudding mix in a mixing bowl and whisk to combine. Add the bread and carefully stir to combine, being careful not to break the bread up too much.

Spray an Instant Pot springform pan with cooking spray, then fill it with the bread mixture and cover with foil. Fill the Instant Pot insert with 1 cup (240 ml) of water. Add a high trivet and top it with the springform pan. Seal the lid and turn the valve to the sealing position. Turn the Instant Pot on manual, high pressure for 40 minutes. Release the pressure manually by carefully moving the valve to venting. Remove the pan and foil and let cool for 5 minutes.

Combine the remaining pudding mix and additional 1 cup (240 ml) of milk and whisk to combine. Place the pudding in the refrigerator to set for 10 minutes. Cut the bread pudding into 6 slices and top with the pudding, sliced bananas and whipped cream if desired.

CINNAMON ROLL BREAD PUDDING

1 cup (240 ml) whole milk
3 eggs
½ cup (110 g) brown sugar
½ tsp ground cinnamon
6 cups (210 g) cinnamon swirl bread, diced into 1-inch (3-cm) cubes, left out overnight

FOR THE GLAZE
1¼ cups (150 g) powdered sugar
3 tbsp (45 ml) milk
¼ tsp vanilla extract

Place the milk, eggs, brown sugar and cinnamon in a mixing bowl and whisk to combine. Add the stale bread and carefully stir to combine, being careful not to break the bread up too much.

Spray an Instant Pot springform pan with cooking spray, then fill it with the bread mixture and cover with foil. Fill the Instant Pot insert with 1 cup (240 ml) of water. Add a high trivet and top with the springform pan. Seal the lid and turn the valve to the sealing position. Turn the Instant Pot on manual, high pressure for 40 minutes. Release the pressure manually by carefully moving the valve to venting. Remove the pan and foil and let cool for 5 minutes.

In a bowl, combine the glaze ingredients. Cut the bread pudding into 6 slices and drizzle with the glaze.

RICE PUDDING

YIELD: 8 SERVINGS

Creamy rice pudding is delicious for a comforting dessert. You can make this ahead of time and reheat it over the stove with about 1 cup (240 ml) of milk. The Coconut-Mango Rice Pudding (page 256) is a play on my favorite Thai dish, mango sticky rice. It's a must-try!

COCONUT-MANGO

CHOCOLATE-STRAWBERRY

ORANGE-MAPLE

PUMPKIN-CRANBERRY

COCONUT-MANGO RICE PUDDING

2 cups (370 g) jasmine rice
2 cups (480 ml) water
1 (13.5-oz [382-g]) can coconut milk
1 cup (240 ml) milk
¼ cup plus 2 tbsp (80 g) granulated sugar
1 tbsp (15 ml) Coco Real Cream of Coconut
Coconut liqueur, to taste (optional)
2 cups (330 g) fresh mango, diced
1 tbsp (6 g) mint, roughly chopped
1 tsp granulated sugar

Place the rice and water in the Instant Pot and seal with the lid. Turn the valve to sealing and turn on manual, low pressure for 12 minutes. Naturally release the pressure for 10 minutes and then stir in the coconut milk, milk, sugar, Cream of Coconut and coconut liqueur, if using. In a bowl, combine the mango, mint and sugar for the topping and let it sit for 5 minutes. Serve over the rice pudding.

CHOCOLATE-STRAWBERRY RICE PUDDING

2 cups (370 g) jasmine rice
2 cups (480 ml) water
2 cups (480 ml) milk
1 cup (200 g) granulated sugar
2 cups (448 g) semi-sweet chocolate chips
1 cup (166 g) fresh strawberries, sliced

Place the rice and water into the Instant Pot and seal with the lid. Turn the valve to sealing and turn on manual, low pressure for 12 minutes. Naturally release the pressure for 10 minutes and then add the milk, sugar and chocolate chips and stir until all the chocolate is melted. Top the rice pudding with fresh strawberries.

ORANGE-MAPLE RICE PUDDING

2 cups (370 g) jasmine rice
2 cups (480 ml) water
1 cup (240 ml) milk
1 cup (240 ml) heavy cream
1 cup (200 g) granulated sugar
Zest of 2 oranges
¼ cup (60 ml) maple syrup, warmed

Place the rice and water into the Instant Pot and seal with the lid. Turn the valve to sealing and turn on manual, low pressure for 12 minutes. Naturally release the pressure for 10 minutes and then stir in the milk, cream, sugar and orange zest. Drizzle the desired amount of warm maple syrup over the rice pudding.

PUMPKIN-CRANBERRY RICE PUDDING

2 cups (370 g) jasmine rice
2 cups (480 ml) water
1 cup (240 ml) milk
1 cup (240 ml) heavy cream
1 cup (200 g) granulated sugar
1 cup (220 g) pumpkin puree
¾ tsp ground cinnamon
½ cup (61 g) dried cranberries

Place the rice and water into the Instant Pot and seal with the lid. Turn the valve to sealing and turn on manual, low pressure for 12 minutes. Naturally release the pressure for 10 minutes and then stir in the milk, cream, sugar, pumpkin and cinnamon. Top the rice pudding with cranberries.

See image on page 254.

CRÈME BRÛLÉE

YIELD: 4 SERVINGS

Crème brûlée is perfectly velvety and elegant. Make sure you try the Chocolate Crème Brûlée (page 261)—it pairs perfectly with some fresh berries and is rich and chocolaty. I especially love the contrast of textures with the creamy custard and crunchy caramelized sugar topping.

CLASSIC

CHOCOLATE

SALTED CARAMEL

LEMON-RASPBERRY

CLASSIC CRÈME BRÛLÉE

2 cups (480 ml) heavy cream
1 tsp vanilla bean paste or vanilla extract
5 egg yolks
¼ cup plus 4 tsp (70 g) granulated sugar, divided
Fresh berries

In a medium-sized saucepan over medium heat, bring the cream and vanilla to a simmer. In a mixing bowl, place the egg yolks and ¼ cup (50 g) of the sugar and whisk to combine until the mixture turns a pale yellow color, about 5 minutes. Add 1 cup (240 ml) of the warm cream to the egg mixture and stir to combine. Add the remaining amount of cream and whisk to combine. Strain the mixture through a fine mesh strainer and place the liquid into a large measuring cup. Pour the liquid halfway up the sides of four 8-ounce (240-ml) ramekins. Cover each ramekin with foil.

Place the trivet into the bottom of the Instant Pot insert. Pour 1 cup (240 ml) of water into the pot and place the ramekins into the pot, stacking them slightly on top of each other if necessary. Seal the lid and turn the valve to the sealing position. Turn the Instant Pot on manual, low pressure for 14 minutes. Naturally release the pressure for 15 minutes, then remove any excess pressure by carefully moving the valve to the venting position. Remove the foil and then place the ramekins into the fridge for 5 hours or overnight.

When you're ready to serve, sprinkle each ramekin with 1 teaspoon of sugar. With a kitchen torch, brûlée the top of the custard by moving the flame over the sugar until it bubbles and becomes golden brown. Let the crème brûlée sit for 1 minute and top with fresh berries before serving.

SALTED CARAMEL CRÈME BRÛLÉE

2 cups (480 ml) heavy cream
½ cup (120 ml) salted caramel
1 tsp vanilla bean paste or vanilla extract
5 egg yolks
¼ cup plus 4 tsp (70 g) granulated sugar, divided

In a medium-sized saucepan over medium heat, bring the cream, caramel and vanilla to a simmer. In a mixing bowl, place the egg yolks and ¼ cup (50 g) of the sugar and whisk to combine until the mixture turns a pale yellow color, about 5 minutes. Add 1 cup (240 ml) of the warm cream to the egg mixture and stir to combine. Add the remaining amount of cream and whisk to combine. Strain the mixture through a fine mesh strainer and place the liquid into a large measuring cup. Pour the liquid halfway up the sides of four 8-ounce (240-ml) ramekins. Cover each ramekin with foil.

Place the trivet into the bottom of the Instant Pot insert. Pour 1 cup (240 ml) of water into the pot and place the ramekins into the pot, stacking them slightly on top of each other if necessary. Seal the lid and turn the valve to the sealing position. Turn the Instant Pot on manual, low pressure for 14 minutes. Naturally release the pressure for 15 minutes, then remove any excess pressure by carefully moving the valve to the venting position. Remove the foil and then place the ramekins into the fridge for 5 hours or overnight.

When you're ready to serve, sprinkle each ramekin with 1 teaspoon of sugar. With a kitchen torch, brûlée the top of the custard by moving the flame over the sugar until it bubbles and becomes golden brown. Let the crème brûlée sit for 1 minute before serving.

*See image on page 258.

CHOCOLATE CRÈME BRÛLÉE

2 cups (480 ml) heavy cream
1 cup (224 g) semi-sweet chocolate chips
1 tsp vanilla bean paste or vanilla extract
5 egg yolks
¼ cup plus 4 tsp (70 g) granulated sugar, divided
Fresh berries, for topping

In a medium-sized saucepan over medium heat, warm the cream, chocolate and vanilla until the chocolate is melted. In a mixing bowl, place the egg yolks and ¼ cup (50 g) of the sugar and whisk to combine until the mixture turns a pale yellow color, about 5 minutes. Add 1 cup (240 ml) of the warm cream to the egg mixture and stir to combine. Add the remaining amount of cream and whisk to combine. Strain the mixture through a fine mesh strainer and place the liquid into a large measuring cup. Pour the liquid halfway up the sides of four 8-ounce (240-ml) ramekins. Cover each ramekin with foil.

Place the trivet into the bottom of the Instant Pot insert. Pour 1 cup (240 ml) of water into the pot and place the ramekins into the pot, stacking them slightly on top of each other if necessary. Seal the lid and turn the valve to the sealing position. Turn the Instant Pot on manual, low pressure for 14 minutes. Naturally release the pressure for 15 minutes, then remove any excess pressure by carefully moving the valve to the venting position. Remove the foil and then place the ramekins into the fridge for 5 hours or overnight.

When you're ready to serve, sprinkle each ramekin with 1 teaspoon of sugar. With a kitchen torch, brûlée the top of the custard by moving the flame over the sugar until it bubbles and becomes golden brown. Let the crème brûlée sit for 1 minute and top with fresh berries before serving.

LEMON-RASPBERRY CRÈME BRÛLÉE

2 cups (480 ml) heavy cream
¼ tsp raspberry emulsion
Zest of 3 lemons, divided
5 egg yolks
¼ cup plus 4 tsp (70 g) granulated sugar, divided
½ cup (63 g) fresh raspberries

In a medium-sized saucepan over medium heat, bring the cream, raspberry emulsion and the zest of 2 lemons to a simmer. In a mixing bowl, place the egg yolks and ¼ cup (50 g) of the sugar and whisk to combine until the mixture turns a pale yellow color, about 5 minutes. Add 1 cup (240 ml) of the warm cream to the egg mixture and stir to combine. Add the remaining amount of cream and whisk to combine. Strain the mixture through a fine mesh strainer and place the liquid into a large measuring cup. Add the zest of 1 additional lemon and stir. Pour the liquid halfway up the sides of four 8-ounce (240-ml) ramekins. Cover each ramekin with foil.

Place the trivet into the bottom of the Instant Pot insert. Pour 1 cup (240 ml) of water into the pot and place the ramekins into the pot, stacking them slightly on top of each other if necessary. Seal the lid and turn the valve to the sealing position. Turn the Instant Pot on manual, low pressure for 14 minutes. Naturally release the pressure for 15 minutes, then remove any excess pressure by carefully moving the valve to the venting position. Remove the foil and then place the ramekins into the fridge for 5 hours or overnight.

When you're ready to serve, sprinkle each ramekin with 1 teaspoon sugar. With a kitchen torch, brûlée the top of the custard by moving the flame over the sugar until it bubbles and becomes golden brown. Let the crème brûlée sit for 1 minute and top with the raspberries before serving.

COBBLER

YIELD: 8 SERVINGS

This cobbler requires only a few ingredients and can literally be dumped in and cooked in a matter of minutes. I love serving these cobblers with vanilla ice cream. This is my go-to easy dessert that I can take straight in the Instant Pot to get-togethers with friends. It stays warm in the pot and travels great in the car.

BERRY

PEACH

STRAWBERRY

APPLE

BERRY COBBLER

20 oz (566 g) frozen strawberries
12 oz (340 g) frozen blueberries
⅓ cup (66 g) granulated sugar
⅔ cup (160 ml) water
1 (15.25-oz [432-g]) box white cake mix
½ cup (114 g) unsalted butter, melted
Vanilla ice cream, for serving

Place the berries, sugar and water into the Instant Pot insert. In a small mixing bowl, combine the cake mix and butter until crumbly. Top the berries with the cake mixture and seal with the lid. Turn the valve to the sealing position. Turn the Instant Pot on manual, high pressure for 10 minutes. Release the pressure manually by carefully moving the valve to venting. Serve with vanilla ice cream.

STRAWBERRY COBBLER

32 oz (907 g) frozen strawberries
½ cup (100 g) granulated sugar
⅔ cup (160 ml) water
1 (15.25-oz [432-g]) box white cake mix
½ cup (114 g) unsalted butter, melted
Vanilla ice cream, for serving

Place the berries, sugar and water into the Instant Pot insert. In a small mixing bowl, combine the cake mix and butter until crumbly. Top the berries with the cake mixture and seal with the lid. Turn the valve to the sealing position. Turn the Instant Pot on manual, high pressure for 10 minutes. Release the pressure manually by carefully moving the valve to venting. Serve with vanilla ice cream.

PEACH COBBLER

3 (15.25-oz [432-g]) cans sliced peaches in heavy syrup, drain 2 of the cans
1 tsp ground cinnamon
1 (15.25-oz [432-g]) box yellow cake mix
½ cup (114 g) unsalted butter, melted
Vanilla ice cream, for serving

Place the peaches into the Instant Pot insert and top with the cinnamon. Stir to combine. In a small mixing bowl, combine the cake mix and butter until crumbly. Top the peaches with the cake mixture and seal with the lid. Turn the valve to the sealing position. Turn the Instant Pot on manual, high pressure for 10 minutes. Release the pressure manually by carefully moving the valve to venting. Serve with vanilla ice cream.

APPLE COBBLER

¼ cup (60 ml) water
2 (20-oz [566-g]) cans apple pie filling
1½ tsp (4 g) ground cinnamon, divided
1 (15.25-oz [432-g]) box yellow cake mix
½ cup (114 g) unsalted butter, melted
Vanilla ice cream, for serving

Place the water into the Instant Pot insert and top with the apple pie filling and ½ teaspoon of the cinnamon. In a small mixing bowl, combine the cake mix, butter and remaining cinnamon until crumbly. Top the apples with the cake mixture and seal with the lid. Turn the valve to the sealing position. Turn the Instant Pot on manual, high pressure for 10 minutes. Release the pressure manually by carefully moving the valve to venting. Serve with vanilla ice cream.

*See image on page 262.

ACKNOWLEDGMENTS

I would like to acknowledge my mother who always encouraged me to pursue my passion for cooking, my husband who is my biggest supporter and fan and my children who are the best little taste testers and non-biased critics.

Thank you to Page Street Publishing for the opportunity to write a book.

And finally, thank you to all of my followers, friends and extended family for encouraging me and supporting me; I am blessed beyond measure.

ABOUT THE AUTHOR

Megan Dow was born and raised in Southern California and started cooking when she was three, baking cookies with her mother every week. Her love of cooking and food has led her to explore many outlets within the culinary world.

Meg is an Italian-trained chef and mom of three. She is the owner and creator of More Momma, a platform to help people cook for the ones they love with the ones they love. More Momma was created in 2018 as a creative outlet to share quick and easy recipes.

More Momma has evolved into a platform to help teach and educate generations to become self-sufficient in the kitchen. Meg is committed to providing easy recipes that the whole family will love through her blog and her cooking school.

Meg graduated from San Diego State University in Hospitality and Restaurant Management and then went to Florence, Italy, for culinary school. She has worked as a private chef, caterer, culinary teacher, restaurant consultant and now runs More Momma full-time.

Her greatest joy is being with her family and cooking with her kids in the kitchen.